Bribery

Steven Zultanski

ISBN 978-1-937027-30-8
Distributed in the USA by SPD/Small Press Distribution
Distributed in Canada via Coach House Books by Raincoast Distribution
Distributed in the UK by Inpress Books

First Edition, First Printing, 2014
Ugly Duckling Presse
232 Third Street, #E-303
Brooklyn, NY 11215

Design by Don't Look Now!
Typeset in Garamond

Printed in the USA
McNaughton & Gunn, Saline, MI
Paper: Roland Enviro Print (100% PCW)
Cover: Mohawk Carnival (30% PCW)

Funding for this book was provided by generous grants from the National
Endowment for the Arts, the Department of Cultural Affairs for New York City,
and the New York State Council on the Arts with the support of Governor Andrew
Cuomo and the New York Legislature.

Bribery

Steven Zultanski

Ugly Duckling Presse
Brooklyn, 2014

The utilization of crime by an artist is impious.
Someone risks his life, his glory, only to be used as
ornament for a dilettante.

— Jean Genet

I F THERE'S ONE THING that's certain for everyone, at all times, no matter where they live or what they obsess over

unreasonably, it's that one can't, at any given moment, get any worse than one already is, without sliding into another

moment altogether.[Of course I'm already awful, but only as awful as I am right now, and just as one holds out hope for tomorrow, knowing it will be better than today, if only because, finally, today will be gone,]I hope when I'm worse

I'll be better too: better, for example, the way women are better than men because they have to put up with men, like saints, while men go around giving the impression they're men, like assholes; better the way poor people

are better than rich people because they take what the rich people hand out to them, like monotonous jobs and fast food and jail time

and work-related bladder cancer; better the way non-white people are better than white people because they aren't allowed to write

the oppressive laws they live under or order the police into their neighborhoods to beat the shit out of their kids; better the way children are better than adults because they're unable to fight back when their parents take out their failures on them; better the way whoever is being bombed right now by American planes is better than the pilots of those planes because they're scattered in more pieces and cover more area; better the way every other person will always be better than me simply by being bigger than me, their thoughts and actions everywhere I'm not — and so on

and so on, one thing is better than another forever, until you die. But for now, if I live even one more day — if this isn't the last time I taste water, sweat through my shirt, squint,

run my tongue over dry lips, find myself unable to speak, cover my eyes — then I won't escape a certain extra degree of dipshit eternity, I'll end up

giving myself at least one more thing to hate about myself, either by doing something I think I dislike, or by doing something I think other people dislike, like committing

some more crimes, which, like the laws they protect, are everywhere at once, written down. There are plenty to choose from. For example, robbing a store at knifepoint.

I did that.

I pulled on a skeleton mask and went with two friends to a little bodega on Bleecker and 4th and we filmed ourselves pushing the clerk into the back room and basically

giving him a hard time and grabbing him around the belly and shaking him as if coins would fall out of his armpits. He was soft and scared and had no idea

we weren't there to hurt him; a few times he even laughed quietly (it sounded more like coughing) when we poked or pushed him, as if he were trying to get in on the joke and play along. At some point he tripped and almost fell over, but I held him up by the arms while he steadied himself. For some reason I expected him to thank me,

which of course he didn't (because I was robbing him), and so I said *thank you* for him, to him, very softly, and he stared at the floor and coughed again, but it didn't sound like laughing anymore. We didn't take much money because there wasn't much

to take and that was fine, we weren't really there for the money anyway, and I mostly regret propping the clerk back up, not because it would have been funny to see him fall — it might not have been — but because

letting him tumble would have been a small enough form of self-relinquishment to make me seem ridiculous

but not quite as terrible as I'd like, because I like to disappoint myself, to make myself sad. It feels good. It would have been

better if I had not only robbed the store and poked the clerk's gut but also pushed him over, if not on his face then at least on his knees, an even more humiliating and suppliant position; this

extra little flourish of cruelty might have granted me a sense of power over him that I didn't want and that he would have expected, but instead I intuitively reconciled my crime to my *sense of self* by

doing something just a little bit nice, and not even nice in a way meant to facilitate the patient savoring of a greater cruelty, like buying a lover

dinner right before abandoning them in the street, but nice in a nice way — though I know the clerk didn't experience my gesture of kindness in terms of kindness, which is a relief. And I can always do something worse, which is also a relief.

Such as: a woman wakes up one morning in her Upper East Side apartment to find deep scratches

dug into her face, and she doesn't know how they got there or remember the pain because there's something mysterious and not entirely of this world about them:

I did that too. And then every subsequent morning

for at least a month she wakes up to find new scratches on her face in different arrangements (one day they're parallel like claw marks, and another day there's a rough triangle carved under her eye, and so on), though never equilateral or particularly rectilineal because

that would be a little too perfect for my tastes and might suggest a kind of technological precision proper to the physical world, as opposed to the raw supernatural barbarism of tearing

at someone's face with your bare hands. But the problem with this crime is that it's generous: the person who endures it might then be convinced that they've been specially chosen

by a divine visitor attempting to communicate with the secular material world through her scratched-up face, a conviction which may

allow my victim to accept her pain stoically. So this is not a particularly good crime to be guilty of, or at least it's not enough on its own, I need

to do something a little less meaninglessly violent, for now, because the very meaninglessness of meaningless violence is inexorably tied to ideals of sacrifice and destiny; in fact, these

ideals (of sacrifice and destiny), insofar as they are pretty much
closed off (at least in their most intimately violent forms, such as
clawing someone's face while they sleep) by our bureaucratized
world, come to appear

as a sort of prehistoric (or otherworldly) good: a sign of the
immediacy and power of primal life, which I don't want anything
to do with.

So how about this: I rob a bank twice.

I just walk into a bank, say, in Williamsburg, with a black baseball
cap pulled down over my eyes, and tell the teller that I have a gun
on me, which I do, and demand

a certain amount of money. The next day, around the same time,
I walk into the same bank wearing the same black cap, approach
the same teller, and demand the same amount of money; it works.
Then I take off

with the cash and stroll a deliberately circuitous path around
the neighborhood. I don't run. I don't hide. I don't do anything
especially violent or anti-heroic. I don't even stare at women in
the street with the sort of intimidatory disinterest which might
retroactively sexualize my robbery, making it into a sign of my
overabundant virility and cool-headed anti-authoritarian suave, the
kind of robbery women supposedly like, not even

that. The whole point is to do something

that no one would like. If I robbed the bank once, everyone would
like it, because there's something romantic about a bank robbery.

After all, banks are dipshits. But by robbing the same bank twice,
I might

convince the public mind, as if there was one, that I'm not a romantic figure. It'll see, as if it saw anything, that I'm a dipshit

freedom from origination

too. Women won't think they like that, and more importantly, men will think they're better than me:

they'll imagine themselves agile enough to refrain from all freely chosen repetition and instead wade in the *river of time* as in an endless series of individuated and originary seconds: never repeating a mistake, never committing the same crime twice in a row, never returning

to the scene of a transgression. It'll give them a sense of superiority, which they'll like, even if they don't

like me. This is basically the same reason a random murder is pointless: it's too simple and unique, you can't do it twice. Let's just

get this out of the way: random murders won't make me worse, so I shouldn't bother to commit them. For example, say transit workers

find two bags on the subway tracks near Columbus Circle. One of the bags is a black trash bag, and inside of it is a blue trash bag. In the blue bag they find the body parts

(not nearly all of them, just a couple) of a young man. The other bag is beige. It's smaller, and full of bloody drill bits and tools. A few

days later, workers at a recycling plant find more body parts inside a blue trash bag stuffed inside a black trash bag. A day after that, they find another black bag containing another blue bag of body parts.

I did this too: I carefully traced the body with a sharp knife before cutting it apart with an electric chain saw. Every cut was clean

and on a joint, indicating that I have a rather conventional and unimaginative knowledge of human anatomy. I hid

the head; it was never found; the cause of death remains unknown. See? I'm not that much worse now. I don't become that much worse simply

by doing something so bad that there's a romantic madness about it. That's not the way it goes: time is complex, as anyone who's ever had a dream knows, it moves in more than one direction.

This is what I do with the head: I wrap it in a big soft white towel as if drying it off and bury it

for hundreds of years, maybe thousands, however long it takes before I feel like digging it up again, or someone else accidentally, half-anthropologically, finds it for the first time. I spread the towel out on my bedroom floor

and place the head near the center of it, or as near to the center

as I care to fix it, by circling the room a few times repeatedly, making centimeter-level adjustments until I'm satisfied. Then

I turn the head on its back, so that the open mouth gapes at the ceiling (I do this because while it's necessary at first to use the relative thinness of the neck to find the approximate center of the towel — seeing as

a smaller point provides us with a more precise measurement — it's too difficult to fold the towel around the head while balanced on its neck· it would probably just tip over, and given that there's no real way to predict whether it would tip this way or that — or if it would bounce, even a little, when it tips, leaving it

somewhere other than the exact center of the towel, as I measured it, admittedly inexactly — it's a better plan to simply turn it

on its side) and I can see into it. The back of the throat

isn't even red anymore, which would have been bad enough, but even worse it's turned kind of black, and the tongue is balled up, like a tiny brain, with a couple of muddy white patches on it, here and there,

like scabs or a bunch of navels, the kind of navels which are a slightly lighter shade of skin than the rest of the belly, even though one expects the navel to usually

look at least a little bit like a hole — a dark tunnel boring into the essences of the body, into the red flesh one never sees, the foundation of things — but that's not how it is: sometimes the navel is all surface, even less deep and enigmatic than the freckled skin of the forearm, say, which doesn't even seem to have a hole in it unless you put one there.

Folding one corner of the big soft white towel at a time, I wrap the prone head perfectly, so that the package

no longer looks like a head, but more like something square and misshapen, the kind of shape which doesn't call any particular object to mind: if there's a generic form of a generic item, it's about the size and shape of a head, but wrapped up. I throw my voice

so that the item seems to talk to me and beg for its life. I'm not trying to be crude, but I figure

if I'm going to do something that other people think is so obvious-
ly bad, I might as well be moral about it. If I get a bit moralistic,
then at least I don't run the risk of simply celebrating whatever
shitty thing I've done, plus I get

the added benefit of being just a little shittier for feigning a
high-and-mightiness about how bad I am. So I ventriloquize
the head begging for mercy, as if I were being doled out a jot of
punishment for my horrendous and unimaginable actions, and I sit
there awhile,

(begging at my own feet) trying not to catch a glimpse of myself
in the mirror doing this so that it's easier to pretend the head lives
independently of my voice, in its own way, as if the begging were
merely a brief episode in the life of the head,

and not even a terribly important one, but just something it felt
like doing for now, out of spite and the pure vital intensity of the
abundant irrepressible will to live. Eventually

I carry my item to the exact center of Prospect Park and start
digging. There's a good reason I'm so intent

on finding the center of things, it's not just a feigned commitment
to symmetry: I need

an element of order to offset the randomness of the murder, be-
cause randomness alone explains itself. Nothing's easier to imagine
than chaos. It's bad enough

that a random murder won't serve my purposes, seeing as it's the
easiest way to mortify everyone at once, myself included. But if a

murder were truly random, it would also be more easily forgiven,
because the blame would turn

impersonal. And this is very personal. I did it, alone. And to prove it, I did it in an idiosyncratic way that played up the relentless specificity of my body: I centered the murdered head

so the rest of the world would seem to revolve around it at all points that I occupied. Millions of years later,

someone or some surviving thing (such as a cockroach with a tiny human brain) will find the head and won't think anything of it; the thing won't know how the head got there and it won't care; there are buried heads all over the place, in every corner of the scorched planet, and nobody worries over their particular histories anymore: nothing revolves

around these heads. The earth is dead. And even if I live another day, and then another and another and another, until the end of time, whatever that means, I'll never do everything I could to these heads; it's impossible to imagine all the awful

things you could do with eternal life. Imagine everything you could give away: you can't. I remember

making a cheesesteak, it was coming along fine, I had already fried the thin strip of meat on the grill and chopped it up with the spatula, poured on the cheese, sautéed

the peppers and onions and mixed them in, flipped the whole thing a couple of times so it would cook

evenly, and squeezed the ingredients into a bun, mashing the slippery greasy bits in with the dull side of a knife. Then I dropped it

on the floor and it landed upside down. My boss looked at me, at the ruined sandwich. He said, Eat it. I said, No. Haha, he said, just kidding, sell it anyway. I said, Ok. He laughed and said, Forget about it, no big deal, just make another one. He was missing

part of his ear. I wanted him to make me sell it anyway so I could hate him, he would have been exactly the kind of terrible

boss he deserved to be, considering that I worked twelve hour shifts and got paid less than minimum wage. Of course he was still terrible, but I resented him for being a little nice sometimes, often when I didn't expect it, which cushioned

my bitterness; sometimes I even laughed at one of his jokes, which were admittedly kind of funny and crude. The point is: if I want to be worse, like a saint or a boss, I need to show

a little bit of love for humanity, so that this little bit of love can be universalized, given to all, and everyone can feel oppressed by it. I need to be vicious in such a basically harmless way that it affirms something

loveable in me. So let's start with something loveable: say I come up with a clever way to steal cell phones, but not too clever. I dress up in nice boring clothes

and approach a stranger on a quiet street. I introduce myself as a policeman and then ask for the stranger's cell phone. It's important not to provide

a reason for my request. Suspicions arise (not to mention fears, both of legal amercement and bodily injury) as soon as

an explanation is given, because the explanation will always be somewhat incompatible with everyday experience and lay knowl-edge of the law's impersonal processes. Similarly, an exaggerated sense of urgency can also trigger distrust. After all, if a policeman were really in such a hurry, he probably wouldn't be ambling down the street in the first place, asking civilians to volunteer their phones. So what I have to do is walk along at a steady pace, eyes straight ahead, searching for a victim in my periphery (I don't want to make eye contact before

the crucial moment when I capture the victim's attention; if we lock eyes too soon, I'll have a harder time parlaying the unsuspecting person's surprise into willingness because he'll have had time, even if just a few seconds, to wonder what it is I want) and, when decided on one, turn

swiftly but smoothly toward him (I wouldn't accost a woman like this, because women are more likely to react unpredictably to a stranger's sudden queries, for good

reason), extending my hand a little, but not quite far enough for a handshake, nor far enough

to softly pat his arm in a comforting gesture meant to signify my relative harmlessness and goodwill,

but just enough to signal a minimal degree of perfunctory social grace, as when someone who waves his or her arms around while explaining something complicated

appears more generous for it, or how a new friend who extends his or her hand a little when interrupting an awkward silence proves to be fluent in the unspoken apologetics which govern the discourse of strangers: even better, I extend

my hand and drop it a little, as if nodding my hand in shame, an almost evolutionary nod, learned into instinct after thousands of years of people getting freaked out when unexpectedly approached by other people, a slight drip of the wrist which not only suggests non-aggression but also the sensual intimacy of a whispered *sorry*, the sheer physicality of self-reproach, the bashfulness of the body in the face of

another sorry body, perhaps similarly softened by embarrassment, or tense and rigid as if expecting to be softened. And so this guy sees

my outstretched hand before his eyes meet mine. By that time his attention

is dispersed: he's focused on me, but not on any particular part of me. For a few crucial seconds, his sight is detached from his understanding. He's taking me in, as it were, but not wholly: I don't

have an identity, a function, or a motive. I'm characterized primarily by the reassuring slope of my hand as it dangles from my arm and the warm fascist steadiness of my eyes, I hope.

I'm a fucking policeman, I say, and I need to borrow your fucking cellphone, quick.

I don't yell, as you can see, but I swear twice. This is key: if I were to yell, I'd scare

the man off, and my abrupt transformation from anonymous pedestrian to aggressive public servant would be so baldly disjunctive that I'd have little chance of being taken for a cop; my behavior

would betray my ignorance as to how exactly a cop acts: of course we must assume that all cops are psychopaths (not just by virtue of a *who-else-would-take-the-kind-of-job-which-involves-repressing-people-often-violently-or-at-least-with-the-constant-and-self-justifying-threat-of-violence* type of logic, but because the job itself creates psychopaths, insofar as it creates people who believe themselves to be the sledge-hammer-esque physical manifestations of an abstract omnipotent law) but this assumption doesn't mean that we know

how this psychopathology appears: in fact,

the assumption that all cops are psychopaths rests on the unpredictability of cops, the feeling of not knowing how they'll respond to any slight stimulus — such as walking past them too slowly, or too quickly, or having

a familiar face, the kind of face his brother-in-law has when he's drunk — which arouses their erratic and discontinuous but nonetheless seemingly personal interest in you, so that no matter what you do, you can't

predict what they'll do, because their actions are self-referential; they don't refer to you even when they are addressed to you, but only back to their own impossible position as the very real agents of an abstract non-entity; the whole paradox here

hinges on the fact that outward erratic behavior is too literal a reading of the unpredictability we're describing: in order to be true to life, I need to act

unpredictably unpredictable, as opposed to the predictable unpredictability of a startling change of character, attitude, or volume. On the other hand, if I asked gently for the phone, I'd seem

like a normal friendly stranger. Hence the swearing, twice. Because if I only swore once it would seem like a nervous performance (what people mean

when they say someone is *trying too hard*, as when one day they wear a different and usually class-aspirational style of clothing, say a particularly nice shirt, and then out of embarrassment — embarrassment over both

the transparency of their aspirations and the depressing obviousness of the self-negation involved in any adoption

of a "new look" — never wear it again), or an aberrational reaction to an exceptional situation, as opposed to a deep-seated or occupational character trait, which is what I'm going for.

The repetition of "fucking" tempers my performance. It's perfect: I normalize

my character's distinguishing trait (his gruff NYPD indifference to politesse in the name

of an omnipresent life-or-death urgency, which comes across more like a craving than a duty) by repeating it,

so that it (the trait) appears (in the instant it's recognized by the victim)

less as a distinguishing trait (which by definition stands out) and more as a generic trait (which by definition doesn't belong to an individual, but to a group, and, as such, to all members of said group), immediately recognizable

and quickly applicable to a broad range of everyday experience, so that there's nothing shocking

about this character, this so-called policeman, speaking in such an unextraordinarily gruff manner about what must be an extraordinary situation. Though of course

there are exceptions to this norm. For example, a policeman was recently arrested for planning to kidnap and cook and eat at least 100 different women.

In any case, I get the cell phone. And then I say, Stay put, a very "cop" thing to say, I think. I tell the owner I'm going to walk

to my car (my police car) to make a call and check whether the phone is stolen. Of course I turn

a corner and vanish, dropping the phone in a public trashcan along the way. That was a pretty good crime. I liked it well enough. The only problem with it was precisely that: I liked it, mildly,

the way I sometimes like bland food, especially when I cook for myself after having been alone all day. Because I didn't have to transgress my own wimpy moral codes (after all, what do I care if a stranger loses his cell phone?) it didn't force me

to consider my next crime, or to regret what I'd done. It was easy to leave behind, as easy as it was for the victim to get a new phone. So I started planning something

slightly bigger, something just a little worse. My first idea

was to invite a conspirator to work with me on the conception and execution of a variant. I figured if two people were to impersonate the police, a much-needed element of intimidation would be added. A second person

would help create the effect of imminent bodily threat, and this might replace the genial coerciveness which had me clumsily balancing

a friendly demeanor with a flat-footed impersonation of donut-headed whiteboy masculinity. This is what happened: a friend and I approached a victim and asked for his ID. See, we decided

to switch it up: instead of demanding a cell phone, which, if two people were asking for it — even if they were policemen — would seem suspicious, a crude ploy to steal the phone, we demanded photo identification, because — even if it's illegal for a cop to randomly ask for ID, which it is — it seemed more like something

that actually happens on a daily basis, or like something that one might expect to happen, at any moment, whenever one sees a policeman or two. The man said

he didn't have his ID with him, he left it at the Econolodge. So we

followed him back to his room, where I said, We're fucking policemen, and you need to show us what you fucking got. We insisted that he had inconvenienced us by roping us into walking all the way to his hotel room; he frowned apologetically

and did exactly what we asked, handed us all the money he had for inspection, which wasn't very much. Given that the amount was relatively small, we claimed to be suspicious

of its authenticity: Listen, we reasoned, we were very busy today, and the only way you convinced us to break our very busy routine and follow you to this stupid hotel room was with the promise (strongly

implied, but never directly stated) of evidence which would be worth our while, and because the only thing

you are showing us here is this money, we have to assume that you're offering it to us as evidence, though perhaps because you are scared for your life or because you don't want to implicate yourself, you are not calling it evidence, and instead you're just

treating it like a gift, or a bribe, or a payment for services rendered;
but we get you, we understand, we know that you aren't simply
handing us this small but nonetheless not entirely laughable sum

of money out of generosity, the goodness of your heart, not only
because you don't know us and have no reason to be so generous
(nor because we don't know you and wouldn't expect such gener-
osity) but also because we know our mere presence here

invokes a procedural behaviorism which, with a stilted formal-
ity characteristic of government workers, flattens all personal
correspondences (such as eye contact, which is the big one, but
also more subtle paranoiac adequations such as comparing the size
of your biceps to someone else's, in this case mine) to functional
contrivances

of the sort one is reduced to in, say, office work (looking your
boss in the eyes to prove the sincerity of your hard work, etc) or
pedestrian hurry,

thereby ensuring that our conversations and transactions in
this hotel room are *all business*, conducted under the aegis of an
officialdom

entirely extensive to the degree that nothing escapes its forced
eudaimonia, an omniscient decorum swallowing every half-
involuntary junkpile of a thought; we're inside of it too, inside
some authority, right here in this hotel room, where you're showing
us this money that we asked for in deference to those social norms
which basically require us

to ask for it, and so we accept your money because we know it's
not really for us, it's not compensation, even though our time and
effort is, you're quite right, valuable, and moreover limited, but this
money

is for the law itself, for its scrutiny and approval: you are basically asking us to check up on this little bit of money, to make sure it's real, to make sure it's not tainted by its role as the mediator of some invisible criminal transaction: we can do that for you, we can go to the station, together if you want, and put this little bit of money through a *special machine* that will determine whether the money is counterfeit or otherwise guilty

of some infraction not directly attributable to the paper itself, of course, but which nonetheless bears on it so fully that it no longer functions as money, it doesn't work, because it no longer belongs to an individual owner but only to the law which protects said owner from the dangers of any guilt or wisdom that it might impart. The effect of this speech was instant. Our victim followed us

into a cab and my friend instructed the driver to take us uptown because, That's where our station is, we said. The driver had been crying. His face was covered in tears. At some point we said, Drop us off here, or Here's good, or Right here, and the cab stopped to let us

out. We stood in a row on the sidewalk as our victim glanced around, presumably looking for the precinct.

It was a dull day, sun-wise. The sky was a dull blue. The buildings were a dull grey. The

pedestrians were dull too, faceless, and they all seemed to be dressed in drab colors, which added

to the general impression that there was not much worth noticing right then — that the entire day, from top to bottom, from high-altitude winds to secret worries, was protecting its anonymity. Even the music from passing cars was not loud enough to make out. It didn't sound like anything. We pushed him into the street and ran away.

As I said at the beginning, I'm already awful. Just look at me. Just look at what I'm doing.

Basically I'm the worst creature that ever existed, a freak of nature that never should have been born. Of course, nothing's worse than an American man, for all the reasons

that everyone already knows: the stupidity, the nationalism, the militarism; the ideological attachment to ideas of independence and comfort; the

donut-headed ignorance of our unimaginably violent and coercive geopolitical power. But I'm the worst kind of American, the kind who criticizes

all these things and benefits from them for the most part fairly unapologetically, or, even worse, apologetically, as in abstractly wishing things were different while diligently working the kind of day job at a non-profit that keeps them exactly the same, or, even worse, not apologetically at all, as when I occasionally involve myself

in a protest movement or activist group and wallow in a brief oceanic feeling of collective universality made manifest in the will of the people while simultaneously wallowing in the knowledge

of this feeling's brevity — because I don't expect the elation of revolt to last, much less the revolt itself — and bask in the aura of dignity offered by its transience: a shitty narcissistic posture badly disguised as communal effervescence. Seriously,

I'm the worst. And that's not good enough for me. I want to be worse. I want this shit country to exist again tomorrow. It's not good enough for me

that we're responsible for the deaths of hundreds of thousands
of people all over the world; it's not good enough for me that we
shoot

scores of people with unmanned drones in Somalia Pakistan
Yemen Afghanistan and claim we do it for our own protection; it's
not good enough for me that we're being poisoned by food

that, like our bodies, is literally shit; it's not good enough for me
that economic sanctions in Iraq Iran Cuba have resulted in the
mass starvation

of the poor; it's not good enough for me that our coercive econ-
omic policies force other nations into debt and austerity; it's not
good enough for me to foster racial hatred and to naturalize

sexual inequality; it's not good enough for me to waste trillions of
hours of billions of lives

in tedious and meaningless and repetitive labor; it's not good
enough for me to burn down the entire planet with

immeasurable tons of bad air; it's not good enough for me to
export our boring corporate entertainment and demand the rest
of the world call it art; it's not good enough for me to cover up a
history of genocide and slavery

with a triumphalist narrative of progress and freedom; it's not good
enough for me to promote "growth" via American investment in
sweatshop labor

in Mexico Haiti China Vietnam Somalia the Philippines and every
other single spot of hot land on the map; it's not good enough for
me to torture

anyone who might resemble an enemy and claim I did it for my own protection; it's not good enough for me to hide thousands of more or less dead souls in secret prisons;

it's not good enough for me to praise the capitalist bitches who hold the horrible world steady as agents of change; it's not good enough for me to hold up

an apartheid state as a model of modern democratic tolerance; it's not good enough for me to blow shit up from far away and call it peace. No. I want more. I want to descend further

into hell. More

hell. I want everything to be worse, and, like a good American, I want it all to start with me, and not with, say, President Obama, where

for a while we can pretend it all starts, and for good reason, because a list of his crimes exceeds all comprehension, it's so long

and multifarious: coordinating with the FBI to plan the assassination of MLK; hiring young thugs

to run over Pasolini; personally driving bulldozers through Palestinian homes; ordering British troops to fire

on Indian revelers at Jallianwala Bagh; dropping Agent Orange on Vietnam; occupying Tibet; sanctioning the crusades; dining on endangered

fish, usually Chilean Sea Bass; nuking Hiroshima and Nagasaki and any future nuked cities; beating Greek

protestors; opening sweatshops in Ethiopia and supervising the toil; handing out pox blankets and slaughtering Native Americans and occasionally even scalping

fellow settlers; buying and selling thousands of slaves; botching
executions and standing idly by while the condemned man writhes
in agony; paying off cartels; manufacturing seeds that grow sterile

after a single generation; and so on. The US president is literally
guilty of pretty much everything: he traverses time and space

with bloody glee, sparing no one and nothing his indiscriminate
wrath, his undifferentiated existential fury

aimed equally at everything extant and not, <u>his unbridled will</u>
<u>to do all the bad he can during his short time in power</u>, to *make*
the most of these eight years such that they subsume all of awful
history. The president

literalizes *human nature* as an overabundance of shitty evil,
and it's in this way that he's a saint: he doesn't exist in a limited
bodily form, he's a time-traveling monstration of spirit, eternally
perfecting himself in the imperfect guise

of another — Obama perfects himself in Bush who perfected
himself in Clinton who perfected himself in Bush who perfected
himself in Washington:

they're all saints. For instance, there was the time that Obama
followed that young man into the subway and kidnapped him (the
same young man that I followed into the subway and kidnapped)
and

brought him back to his apartment and chopped him up into little
pieces with a bunch of different saws, each designed for a different
kind of cutting and thus proper to different parts of the body:
handsaw for soft flesh, jigsaw for cartilage, bonesaw for bone, etc.
He began by cutting strips of flesh away from the bone

with the handsaw and laying these strips side by side on an enormous thick white towel. Then he took the bonesaw and sawed through any joints he felt like sawing through: knees and elbows and hips and shoulders and some little joints in the fingers and toes. You could tell he liked it because

the decision about which joints to saw seemed, from an outside perspective, arbitrary: there was no method to the operation, just the pleasure of discovery. Eventually

he cut the head off. Big thick bubbles of blood burbled out of the neck, which is what happened when I did the same thing. Then he delicately stacked

the cut-up chunks of flesh on strips of skin and balanced the torso on top, as if the victim were curled up sleeping

on a pile of himself. Taking one corner at a time, he folded the towel and tied the body parts up in a bundle. The bundle

fit inside a black garbage bag, which then fit inside a bigger blue garbage bag. (This is the big difference between how he and I committed the same crime: he neatly bound everything up in one bag, while I tossed all the pieces

haphazardly into a number of different bags, though I used the same blue/black combo.) And we've already seen how he makes the head talk and buries it in the park. All that's the same, it's just what I would do. It begged him for mercy too.

But as I said, that's not enough. It's not enough

to know that our overlord shares my guilt, or even to know that he's guilty of all crimes ever committed (unlike me: I'm not guilty of everything: I'm just a little finite shithead, not a great big omnipotent shithead), because his guilt can't get any worse, nor can it appear as the worst, a condition which at least has the dignity of transience. After all, one can't be the worst forever. The president's guilt is different: it never changes, nor is it muffled by the screams of new victims: his crimes are always everywhere at once

in exactly the same way forever: they are not distinctive enough to be various: his crimes are all part of one enormous crime, and one crime, no matter how

enormous, is never enough. His is the same white blur haunting the edge of every periphery. My crimes, on the other hand, are many. Infinite, like the night. Each of my awful acts is awful in itself, and not by virtue of a greater awfulness which

accounts for and murmurs the individual parts. And so even if I'm already perfectly the worst creature that has ever existed, which I am, the time between my separate acts of unhappy conscience ensures their sequence

as a narrative: one comes after another. They are necessarily chronological, and each one will appear to comment on and/or escalate the previous entries in the series, so that

I seem to change over time, and my actions are not merely the expressions of an essential character but rather the effects of a mutation. For example, even if my last crime wasn't good enough to make me as bad

as I'd like to be, the next crime I commit, no matter how petty, will cause its predecessors to worsen, simply because it will be a continuation of something that was already bad.

It was dark. I knew that her basement windows were unlocked because I had checked all the houses on this street and hers were open every night; either she was careless or she was waiting for someone to sneak in, like me. I crept up the stairs to the first floor, careful not to let the chain

rattle or drag along the stairs. When you're walking slowly on a level surface, you can shuffle forward quietly, but when you're walking up a staircase, especially an old long wooden one with high steps, you have to raise

your foot fairly high and then bring it clacking down again on the next step, many times over, so that if you want or need to make this trek silently,

you have to lift your feet painfully slowly and drift them down equally slowly, and even more slowly right before they meet the stair. This isn't difficult, but it's harder to do

while carrying a chain. Your body vibrates and shakes. You stand on one foot, slowly lowering the other, tempted to stamp down quickly, as if

squashing a bug, to regain balance, but because the whole point of creeping slowly up the stairs is to not stamp down quickly, you have to hold

this position for a few seconds longer (say, three or four seconds) than you otherwise might, and those few seconds are subjectively lengthened by a mild but quickly intensifying tremor, which you would think you would feel

most acutely in the burdened leg, but you don't, you feel it in your arms, which are cradling a heavy chain, and you can't allow them, your arms, to tremble too violently

for fear of waking the homeowner with the clinking of the chain, so you squeeze them, your arms, tightly around the chain. So I squeezed

So you, So I

my arms around the chain. But I squeezed so hard my muscles were twitching and I could feel

myself losing control of my reflexes, and the only way to subdue the involuntary minor convulsions that were about to cause me to drop the chain was to relax a little, for a

half-second or so, and this half-second of relief gave me the necessary extra strength to hold myself steady for another few seconds while I pulled my other foot up to the next stair, and while I did that I found

that it was already there — my foot was already on the stair and I was already balanced again, my step had landed silently without my piloting it. I was distracted

by my upper body and my feet kept on without me. I guess the only way I can do something like this, the only way I can break into this woman's house while she's sleeping and leave a chain stretched across the floor

as a kind of cipher — of what I don't know and more importantly she won't know either — is if my body doesn't so much obey as follow me, or I it, without having to consciously manage every twitch and step: I can only do it without me, to some extent. In any case, I found myself in the kitchen, as good a place as any to

leave the chain. I pushed a chair to the center of the room. I slowly unrolled

the chain and tied one end around a leg of the chair, and then, crawling like a baby, stretched the rest

of it across the floor, pointing toward the front door, because that seemed like an ominous thing to do, suggestive of ritual and/or some kind of obsessive logic that could be paranoiacally interpreted by whoever finds it. My knees shook as I stood up again.

It's obvious that this incident, by itself, isn't really so bad.

But you can see how it reacts with my other crimes. For example, even if we agree that stealing cell phones is

not exactly behavior indicative of someone irredeemably awful, because lots of people are doing worse things all the time — right now Obama is probably

pulling someone's fingernails off or tasering a naked prisoner — and that breaking and entering, while worse than ripping off cell phones, is hardly a big-picture atrocity (and while it's certainly intensely creepy

to leave chains lying around in ritualistically suggestive poses, it's also not as bad as, say, feeding a detainee on hunger strike by forcing a tube up his nose and down his throat and then while the foodstuff

is being drained into his body yanking the tube from side to side until tears are streaming down his gaunt, starving face), you have to admit

that many bigger crimes make more sense, they fit into a legible ideological and technocratic structure, while my particular style of worsening simply makes less sense: it's harder to attribute all my actions to one identifiable person or intention — even though

I did it all, very much on purpose — and, as such, a certain sympathetic parentalism (as in, *how could my son do something like this, he's always had a big friendly smile for everyone he met*) becomes inapplicable

or at least very hard to apply, because I no longer seem like
anyone's son: I can't blame everything

on my father or my father's father. Granted, they've probably done
some pretty bad things,

and I'm not suggesting they deserve to be exonerated because my
own dipshit misadventures have rendered me unrecognizable. I
don't know exactly

what they've done. My father was in Vietnam, for example, and
even though he says he didn't fire a gun there, at least not at a
human body, I'm sure he did some other things, necessarily, that
one might count

as bad, or terrible, and it's possible to count his simply being there,
even if it was more or less against his will, as a terrible thing,
considering that anything he did or was ordered to do was part of
a larger

campaign to firebomb a whole people into floating white ash while
they were eating dinner or watching their children sleep or fighting
back. And my grandfather flew a bomber in WWII. He blew
people up. Not to mention the investments that have made

them each a little money. Those are probably bad. Whatever
companies jumped in value and bought them retirements and paid
for their children's educations

have certainly been involved in some evil shit; at the very least,
those companies underpaid their employees or covered up a couple
of cases of thyroid cancer

at their offshore factories. But it doesn't matter. It doesn't matter
what sort of minor world-historical crimes my father has committed

— crimes which have contributed to my all-pervasive shittiness and well-being. Even if he had simply and involuntarily

perpetuated the oppressive patriarchal norms of our sexist society by, say, asking my mother to wash the dishes more often than he washed them, or, even worse, acted like

a total asshole and washed the dishes every night before my mother could even offer because he didn't want to be the kind of man that asked his wife to wash the dishes more often than he did, and then

resented her for it, I would still be terrible. It's not his fault. And it's not my mother's fault either, for being a saint, because

even if there's nothing worse than saints, it's nonetheless the case that anyone can be one, everyone is given things by assholes and accepts them, and so everyone potentially

manifests boundless love in their fragile human bodies, regardless of what they do. Doing is not

essential to sainthood. Sure, my mother must have done some saintly things, such as having

me, for example, or letting my father pay for a meal even though she was perfectly capable of paying for herself, or smiling when she was supposed to think

I said something cute. But those things don't count. As the inheritor of a tradition of inheritance, one has a duty to take and to hate taking, at which point

the offering, quivering with hate, becomes unstable, like a fist trembling with anger that misses its target and swings through dead air. This is why I need to be generously given my crime — that is, offered my freedom to commit a crime, or to own up to it — so as to shatter

my designated ownership of it, so that I can hate it twice: once for being mine, and once for being

someone else's to give away. Lucky for me, all crime is gifted or none of it is, and I can assume that everything I've done has been bestowed on me: after all, I didn't invent

anything. My crimes, like all crimes, are unoriginal. I remember a neighbor girl shoving her cat in a bucket

and swinging the bucket around her head. We were more impressed by the power of gravity to keep the cat safely in the bucket

than we were by the cat's impassive attitude toward the game. It was probably stunned, paralyzed with fear. Other people have done that. She wasn't the first to swing a cat in a bucket; she couldn't have been. I must have done it too. I don't remember

not doing it. Your crimes are already there. You've already committed them. You've already repented. You've already been forgiven and then done it again, whatever it is that you've done. Only when you begin committing all the crimes in the world

does it seem like no one is offering them to you; later it seems like each one is merely another present to unwrap — and not even the kind of present that makes your heart beat faster for having received it, a present from an estranged lover who may or may not be giving you something as a sort of revenge, say, but more like

a present dropped in your office mailbox by your boss, which turns out to be a gift certificate to a restaurant owned by the company you work for.

I hate that company. Of course I hate it. I hate all capitalists and their dipshit banks, though I admit

they save our terribleness for us, so we can redeem it later. They keep it safe, kind of in the form of gift certificates. You can have whatever you want; the awful world is overflowing with riches and rape. It's everywhere. It's

protected. Every fraternal organization is built on riches and rape. Businesses, mafias, churches, police unions, fraternities, political parties, armies, rock bands, militias, hunting clubs, secret societies: too many

to name, and all working together, more or less, to force compliance. For example, we can take it as a given that many male professional athletes in the US are rapists, no matter what sport they play: football, tennis,

hockey, mixed martial arts, baseball. Everyone knows this. Everyone knows, when they watch a game of corporate

sports, that they are rooting for rapists, cheering them on. How do we know? Not just because male professional athletes in the US are indicative of a culture of rape in which masculine aggressivity is rewarded

with sympathy and monetary success and widespread respect and sometimes outright idolization so that our millions of desolate men wake up every day

feeling like they're in charge of their lives; and not just because professional sports elevate brute muscular physicality to the level of art so that beating the shit out of someone becomes one of the only legitimated forms of self-expression or creative work in a world where no one is free or creative; and not just because the aforementioned outright idolization of male professional athletes in the US serves a pernicious educational function and teaches boys

the value of the aforementioned aggressivity; and not just because women's roles in professional sports are usually sexualized in the most

degraded way and not even in the degraded-in-a-sexy-way kind of way but just the sad kind of degraded, and not the sad-kind-of-degraded-that's-also-degraded-and-sad-in-a-sexy-way either; and not even simply because there have been so many male professional athletes in the US who've been convicted

in assault cases and/or for whom it's been revealed that someone or some organization was covering up: none of these reasons are personal enough

to secure our knowledge. We know because we cover up for them. We pretend that they aren't rapists. We pretend

that the reported instances of sexual violence are merely aberrations against a background of normal peaceful behavior, even though

the normal behavior of male professional athletes in the US has never been

peaceful. Let's add them up, like numbers: the players involved in campus rapes covered up by universities; the players involved in rapes covered up by their respective professional/corporate associations; the players treated

to dubiously voluntary prostitution by their team owners as a sort of luxury compensation or bonus; the players involved in covering up for other players at either a university or professional level; the players involved in covering up for those players who are covering up for other players; the players

who don't remember assaulting anyone and think of themselves as innocent; the players who don't know or want to know

what rape even is and so don't believe that, for example, sex with someone who is too drunk to consent qualifies as rape; the players who believe that their celebrity itself

qualifies as a sort of consent; and so on. If one adds all these shitheads together, the number of rapists and accessories to rape

is even higher than the number of players. There are literally more male professional athletes in the US that are rapists than there are male professional athletes in the US. (This fact is literal

because it's symbolically fixed as part of a pattern, so that even if not all parts of the pattern fulfill the same function, they nonetheless compose the same big picture — or, in this case, the same

endless horror — which can be understood as a single idea despite the irregularities of particular pieces. This is also why the recent colloquial misuse of "literally" is more correct than grammarians and

English professors can know: it's a conversational means of marking those things that, in their rudimentary universality, have been stripped of their numerical or rational exactitude to become more generally sort of true, and thus literal. Think of the

pomegranate. The pomegranate

works as a symbol of the female sexual organ even though it doesn't "resemble" said organ; moreover, the variety of seeds in an individual pomegranate — not to mention across pomegranates — means that there will always be more than a few seeds that don't seem

as if they can be integrated into this image: instead of slippery red fruits that slick your fingers with slime, like the thin film of menstrual radiation that sheaths one's body after messy period sex, some seeds

are green and hard and dry. But all women's female sexual organs are not the same either, and not even

a single woman's female sexual organs are the same all over. There are variations in epidermic and mucosal chroma; there are over-saturated patches

too deep to drink from and irritated hair follicles that she asks you to avoid licking because saliva makes them burn; there are different textures —

for example, slightly bumpier and slightly smoother — within the breadth of a single distal phalange. In this way, the disparateness of a pomegranate's seeds is a literalization

of its sexualization, which is analogous to the irregularities of the body. So that people all over the world, when they split a pome-granate open like a skull and the juice

splashes dark purple spots on their nice white clothing and they slide a few fingers in and gently loosen

the seeds and tear at the pink flesh of the fruit, people all over the world, at this moment, imagine a woman's small real penis — though the pomegranate, obviously, also looks like brains. Similarly, when I say that there are more male professional athletes in the US that are rapists than there are male professional athletes in the US, I mean it. It's just true.)

Which is what disgusts me about my male friends' attempts to better themselves by feigning a libidinal (or, even worse, intellectual) investment in

professional sports. They know

exactly what they're doing. They know that corporate sports entertainment is deeply complicit with a culture of rape and is partly responsible

for a version of masculine identity founded on aggression and competition. And yet

they want to feel united with others, they want to be *one of the guys*, they want to preserve the illusion that the consumption of this particular form of entertainment connects them to millions of strangers, all unimaginably

different, who are consuming the same thing and basking in the same brief feeling of unity. And I admit it:

I did that too. I wore a hat. I walked slowly while a friend followed at a discreet distance. I kept my eyes on the ground and my friend

did the looking for me. When he spotted a potential victim he threw his voice

and made it sound as if I throbbed a soft *hello* in the woman's general direction. This part was important: in order that she wouldn't run (or, even worse, emit the kind of hiccupy grunt that serves as an obligingly minimalist disacknowledgement of an overfriendly male presence) the greeting had to come from something not exactly me — the idea was, if it seemed to arrive not quite from my mouth

but from the empty air around me, maybe she wouldn't preemptively perceive me as the threat that I think

I am. Staring at my feet (so that when her eyes landed on mine they'd also move down to my feet and away from my face), I swung

into her, hugging her face to my chest with one arm and holding her head there with the other. Her dark hair fell relatively straight, though it was wavy behind her ears. Her mouth opened and wet

the front of my shirt, but the moisture didn't seep through to my chest. I locked my legs, so that if she tried to twist away I'd be planted

firmly against her gyrations. She didn't gyrate. We held each other perfectly still, like when one soap bubble running down a shower curtain collides with another bubble and they absorb each other, and you know

that this new heavier bubble is about to slide down but there's a moment in which it just hangs there as if waiting to see how heavy

its new body is before surrendering to physics. Or you poke it and the bubble bursts. Her saliva

trickled down her chin, and a dot of it landed on the toe of my shoe. We both looked at it. It just sat there, dissolving into the leather. In a few seconds

it was gone. And then my friend, whom I had momentarily forgotten about and whom the woman never knew about, wheezed for me — that is, he threw his voice so that it sounded like I wheezed — to remind us, I suppose, of our

immediate material purpose, of the decidedly now-or-never-type business at hand. But as I've already made clear, a single crime, even if in communion with all my previous single crimes,

is not enough to continue making me worse; besides, if rape is committed all the time without comeuppance by our cultural heroes, it certainly isn't good enough for me. She scratched me across the face and ran. Blood was streaming out of my mouth, though I don't remember getting punched. I decided

to give up, but it occurred to me that even if I failed, I was still pretty bad: harassing women on the street is a shitty thing to do, and maybe the perfect crime

for someone who wants to be worse. It's not as awful as rape, but it's still irredeemable. Of course, I'm not attempting to claim that I'm not a rapist, as if there were one crime I could not bring myself to commit, or write about. After all, I've committed lots of crimes at least once, and many of them

more than once. But sometimes one hits upon a variation that's even more counterintuitively criminal and horrific than the original idea, the one in law books and novels.

We walked slowly. It was cold. It seemed like it might rain, but didn't. We weren't

the only people on the street. I had no idea

where we were, which was exactly what I was looking for. At some point I motioned with a limp directional wave and my friend obediently hid behind a tree. I hid behind another, close by but far enough away that my plan, which required concentration, wouldn't be compromised or diverted by anything he might whisper or moan. We waited. Eventually a woman came towards us, alone, looking around, as if searching

for us, or something like us. I thought it would be worse if I pictured what I was about to do before I did it, so that it would feel both more premeditated and more inevitably disappointing

when it didn't live up to my expectations: I pictured her blank face focused on something in the distance, or on nothing at all, as I crawled

out from behind my little tree and grabbed her wrist lightly; I imagined it would feel like her hand was passing through an otherworldly mist, a portal

to another dimension for hands, in which perhaps they're independent of their bodies and make their own ghostlier decisions to walk on fingertips across the ceiling and wrap themselves around the guilty throats of the living, etc; and I imagined she must have felt

trapped, not so much trapped by anyone in particular but trapped between worlds, a place from which you can't even wave away an accosting presence in the physical world because

part of you is floating around in the other world; and I imagined that as she slowly came to whatever passes for full awareness of this particular world and its particular threats, I whispered

to her, as quietly as I could, something to the effect of *I want to roll your sweet hard seeds between my blood-red fingers and taste your small real penis in my mouth*, a carefully chosen sentence by which I tried to cast a sort of iron spell, an attempt to transport her, cell by cell, to the ghost-world; her unflappable urban attitude dissolved and she found

herself empty of reflexive content, with nothing to say in response to the freshly visible other side of the terrible phenomenal world: she knew she was about to be attacked by a ghost, but she didn't know what, if anything, to think about that. The only thing she could do was bury

her head in my comforting chest and slowly raise her eyes to my blank face and drool down my shirt.

As you can see, my imagination failed me. I found that I couldn't quite bring myself to picture the specifics of the crime, much less the specifics of her person, but only the

contours of our noumenal bodies in existential struggle, so that when she got close enough for me to actually see her human features, they startled me not because

they differed from what I had imagined, but because they existed at all. This threw me off. I lobbed myself out from behind the tree with the kind of gentle stumble that suggests harmless city drunkenness, and when I grabbed for her

hand, to pull it into ghostly limbo, she retracted it without so much as a flinch — she simply passed with a disinterested swerve. My hand felt heavy and fleshy. It fell

to my side. Stepping out behind her, I desperately attempted to recover

the spirit of my endeavor by enunciating the magic words, which I expected, even if they didn't have the binding effect I had originally intended, would at least provoke her to turn around, to look directly at me and perhaps through me. I could work with that, that would be something. But no: I spoke nervously and quickly, not at all like a ghoul or a warden of souls, but exactly like the very human kind of sad drunk that one learns to ignore; you don't

even hear it anymore, because you've heard so much similar nonsense that it no longer surprises. I might as well have asked her for a quarter

for the bus. She walked on. My friend behind the tree began to whimper and moan. Maybe he liked what he saw

as her resistance to my advances, I don't know. His moaning grew louder. I knew the woman definitely wasn't going to turn around now, with one voice behind her whispering sweet nothings about her unnaturally juicy pomegranate and another voice moaning like a hungry puppy.

I breathed it in.

I pushed off

into a pretty swift little gallop. I thought the swish of my voracious approach (at least, I wanted it to sound voracious, like a tiger's pounce) would trigger

a shriek, or some quieter sign of fear. It didn't, but just before reaching my prey — it didn't take long, she hadn't sped up — I dodged left, then right,

then left again, or something like that (the directions aren't actually important, it was basically just a zigzag), and, in one last burst of inspiration, circled around

in front of her and came to a sudden halt. Face to face. At last she knew it: I wasn't a ghost, which she never thought I was. And she might have been finally

about to shriek when a would-be do-gooder that neither of us had
noticed addressed me with, What's going on here?, or some such

hackneyed hero-speak. Now, as I've been incessantly repeating, I
wish I were worse. And wishing to be worse is a long and painful
ongoing personal project, like yoga or chemotherapy: it's not as if
you just start out

one day and the next you can stand on your head or live another
three months. And part and parcel of such personal projects is

the need for quick thinking, for the kind of in-the-heat-of-the-
moment decision that radically alters the bend of the internal path
that you had convinced yourself you were following. I immediately
decided that these two

were offering me something cheap and invaluable: the opportunity
to make one into a hero and the other into a lucky victim, while
worsening my own shitty life

through a mild exaggeration of my evil intentions. I sucked it in.
The gallant stranger shuffled a half-step forward, a move presum-
ably meant to intimidate but which instead betrayed

the caution that he probably thought he had abandoned to
courage. I made a fist as if ready for whatever was coming and
unconcerned about what

it might be. We played our parts perfectly. But before he could
hesitate or reconsider his spontaneous display of dashing masculine
nerve, I jabbed

him in the nose. It was a pretty weak jab, as jabs go, and it
probably surprised me more than it surprised him,

because I wasn't really expecting to throw it, while he, for obvious reasons, most likely expected

something more or less like it. And the way I dealt with my own startlement was to turn quickly to the woman ostensibly being rescued and to jab her too, also

in the nose, twice, the second time as a kind of quick-thinking stab at convincing myself the other punches

weren't merely accidental or thrown out of sheer muscularity, almost as involuntary self-defensive reflexes in which my arms leapt off my body to protect their bearer and

neutralize its enemies. I definitely freaked everyone out. They must have known now that I meant to do them physical harm, and that I was prepared to snap

their bones in two. But even if they knew this, and even if the woman who I punched in the nose twice was standing there

pinching her bloody nostrils together between her thumb and index finger and

softly sobbing, even then it wouldn't be enough — the fact that I was a total stranger meant

that my threatening pose could too easily be absorbed into a logic of so-called mental illness: I would seem

to them as if I had a certain sort of unstable brain, and this malfunctioning brain, because

of its lack of awareness regarding its own malfunction, would function as a murmurous apology for these punches which I couldn't seem to control: if I came off as insane — intentionless, animal, acting out

impulse — my victims might have felt sorry for me. So in order to convince them otherwise — to convince them that my harassment was not arbitrary (wrong place at the wrong time sort of thing)

or involuntarily surrealist (driven by the apocalyptic collapse of dream and reality), but a premeditated assault — I had to tell them

exactly what I was about to do to them, and why. Which is what I did. In just a few words. Then I ran. I doubt my short speech had the intended effect, but

that's not important. The important part of becoming worse is trying to become worse: it's immaterial as to whether each shitty thing I do is quite as shitty as I would like it to be.

For example, it didn't go nearly as well as I had hoped when I stalked a little boy for a few months.

Don't worry, I wasn't caught. That wasn't

the problem. Though I wouldn't have resented getting caught, since it would have been awful. And besides, the boy never found out I was stalking him, despite my brazen escalations of the pursuit. At first I wasn't surprised that I went unnoticed. After all,

little boys are kind of stupid, most of the time they're more or less oblivious

to what's happening around them unless it directly involves their vaginas: they couldn't be more attentive to the warm chill shivering through their fingertips when they spread

their smooth hairless pussy lips as they sit down to pee, for instance, and they savor the porcelain seat's radiating coolness as it streams over

their ass and disappears into their thighs. But they don't notice things like strange adults, even when the strange adults are doing something that

involves them and is potentially sexual in nature. In any case, there was nothing sexual

about my stalking of the boy. I simply walked to his school in Park Slope every day at 3pm when classes were dismissed

and waited for him to pass with his friends. That was all. I just watched him from the window of the coffee shop where I pretended to be reading

a novel, or occasionally something more ascetic than a novel, like a treatise of some sort, as cover. There was no particular reason I chose this particular boy. There was nothing special

about him, and he didn't stand out, even to me. I was fixated, though I couldn't even clearly picture his face. In fact, after weeks of watching him, it still took me a few minutes to pick him out of the scrambling, screeching, conspiring crowd of children

to which he artlessly belonged. But my choice wasn't random, either: he just happened

to stroll into the coffee shop while I was listlessly reading, and his chirpy laugh inspired a new thought. Subtracted from his body, his voice dipped back

behind his mouth, as if someone, say myself for instance, were throwing my voice into his, in a mock childlike squeak, so that he might be spoken through. This slight auditory distortion, by which

I momentarily misplaced his voice in my own so that I heard mine in his, redirected

my attention entirely to the space between us. Lodged there was a possibility: I could get a little worse if I crossed that

gulf. It's easy. Like breaking into a thickly carpeted house. Inspiration is a funny thing, because it beats you

to whatever you were racing toward, and then mocks you from behind when you think you've caught up; you're too late: the end of the line has been moved further along, or behind you, or somewhere to the side. The point is that there's something

about inspiration that's fundamentally uncalled for, unsought by the person overturned by its affections and yet tethered to the will: a deadly swerve

unattributable to the conscious wishes or internal narration of the driver, who didn't expect to turn the wheel so suddenly, but just as unattributable to road conditions or mechanical malfunction. The driver saw

something in the road or felt something in the vibration of the car that he or she didn't expect to see or feel, and attended to it in a way that he or she could not have imagined attending to it, and this

changed everything. In this case, an aural illusion (the sound of my voice in the boy's laugh) distracted me from the half-perceived trickle

of dim thought winding its way through that particular moment, and occasioned an unforeseen, interruptive idea: *I will stalk this boy for the remainder of his childhood.* As long as he stays irresistibly indifferent to those immortal adult figures lurking in his periphery, I'll be one of them, I thought.

So I was one of them, for a time. I didn't change, at first, what I had been doing, since it worked. I didn't

move. I scanned the street from the coffee shop. I watched the children as they wandered out of sight. It must have looked like I was daydreaming. I daydreamed. I reflected on

my own boyhood, and basked in the feeling of belated guilt for those little shitty things I did then that I didn't feel guilty about at the time: the time

I rummaged through my parents' dresser drawers and thought about taking some money I found but didn't; the time I pulled my hair out until I bled from the scalp and then told my parents my sister did it. Soon the street was empty and I left the café

and began to follow the small group of giggling children, one of whom would sometimes burst out in a shriek. I guess that's what kids do. They occasionally shriek. I didn't need

to hide. No one was watching and I didn't look suspicious. There was nothing about the pace of my stride or the flashing intensity of my eyes that would have given me away. Adults usually

appear to be drowning in the flood of their neurotic thoughts as they walk, that's what adults are like. And so I only needed to do what I already would have done

in order to do what I wanted to do: I self-obsessed. This worked, not only on the first day of stalking, but on all the subsequent days when I did the exact same thing. There were many days like this. They were all alike. I learned nothing more about the boy (whom I knew nothing about in the first place), though I felt

us grow closer. As far as I know he never noticed me. He never even glanced half-meaningfully behind him. By the time the season changed we were stuck with each other, our days linked, gridded, like a fence or a certain kind of painting. Each afternoon resembled the last, except

in weather and mood. Little boys, after all, oscillate unpredictably between hyperactive outbursts of manic vocalization, like shriek-ing, and blissful narcissistic silent brooding, and this particular boy (who, as I hope I've emphasized, had no particular qualities attributable to him that couldn't also be attributed to

other boys his age: I refused to come close enough to see his face or make distinctions, because such distinctions would have ruined everything, they would have given the whole affair

an air of the personal, and in that case I may be forgiven or at least shown some pouty sympathy for my involuntary attachment to the boy, who, even if underage and unaware, somehow riveted himself to me

so tightly I couldn't unfasten myself, at least not without help), being more or less just like other boys, did the same. One day he was laughing and playing, and the next he was

hanging his head and slouching lumpish ten feet behind his classmates (which meant that I had to do the same, slouch slowly along, so as not to catch up with him). And then one day

he was just gone. He didn't exit the school, and his friends walked home as if nothing were missing from their lives. I didn't bother following them. This went on

for a while before I got the hint. I returned the next day, and the next, under the assumption

that whatever boyhood ailment (24-hour stomach bug, flu, mono, belated second chicken pox) had afflicted him, it wouldn't last long. Of course I never found out whether sickness

was the cause of our separation, or if something else happened. He never showed up again, and I eventually stopped

wishing he would; it was easier to move on to something else. I immediately saw that I had made a mistake, and that this mistake didn't worsen me as dramatically as I would have hoped, which was perfect: while I was right to keep my distance and to insist on the impersonal tenacity of stalking, without

relying on shopworn psychological narratives or prefabricated justifications, I nonetheless missed

a chance to dazzle myself with an unforeseen attachment to the very thing I was supposed to (by my own orders) remain yawn-ingly unattached to: if I had begun to want

the boy (in the sense of wanting to do something to him, for example grazing his hairless freckled arm as I brushed past) then not only would I have appeared to be worse in the eyes of those for whom wanting this boy in any little way is

feigned unthinkable, but I also would have betrayed my moment of inspiration by following a new path which I knew led away from my stated aim. And while sometimes a swerve

away from an aim is a sign of worsening, it can just as often be an improvement over a path that was originally worse to begin with. For example, say a saint

doesn't die. Instead of being stoned to death, or burned at the stake, or slowly bled from his or her shredded fingers after his or her fingernails have been torn off, he or she simply keeps on living, and continues doing so for as long as his or her body holds out. In this case the saint is made better than he or she otherwise would have been, because saints are the worst and if saints live a little longer than they should they'll have more time to be the worst: redeeming

the awful things other people do, transforming hate into love, forgiving others for things that should not be forgiven, like being a saint. So if I had begun to want the boy I was stalking, I would have veered from

the path I had set out for myself, and this would have made me both better and worse at the same time: better because I had betrayed my inspiration (and worse for the same reason), and worse because I allowed desire to trump inspiration (and better for the same reason). There's a lesson here

about worsening: nothing is worse than love. Of course my desire to touch the boy's arm, if I had such a desire, which I didn't, could in no way be confused with love. But

retroactively it could have been taken for the first sign of love, the founding gesture of a lifelong, or, even more dramatically, an eternity-long

attachment, an unbreakable bond which, much like the US president's life, spills over

its initial site of reality (in this case, those few seconds of arm-brushing) and into everything else around it, all those other empty unreal sites brushing against it,

like men. Men are shitty and sad. Sometimes they don't die, they just get shittier and sadder, forever. The president is just an exceptional man, like other men but more so. He does more of the same terrible things that other men do and have done, plus his own unique terrible things: he also wanted to brush the boy's arm, and so he did and fell in love. The years ahead were filled with memories

of this contact, and Obama's every lusty sniff of his boy-lover's pungent little deferential armpit (or perhaps girl-lover's, because as I've said he and I are not exactly the same, there are any number of slight but crucial differences in our histories and futures which maintain the meaningful distinctness of our names) while cuddling in the late morning,

sheathed in a thin film of night's sweat, legs woven together in summer warmth, almost too warm for comfort — each deep familiar sniff called back to that one first peachy light touch, the unforgettable

but insignificant inspiration for love, remembered repeatedly, and with each recollection renewed and faded.

Love too lasts forever, which is why it's awful. And it lasts forever precisely insofar as it is always comparative: one returns

to the initial encounter and consciously or not compares the present encounter to it; in this way everyone's fears of being stacked up

against their former selves (*Is my body less attractive now that it's familiar? Is my hair falling out more quickly or is that the usual rate at which hair falls out? Does she like the grey in my beard or does it remind her of her father? Am I more*

irritable or irritating, or both, than I used to be? Are my jokes still funny? Were they ever funny or was she pretending to laugh because she wanted someone to like her and the fastest way to someone's heart is to flatter them with laughter?) are not only completely rational, but routinely actualized by both partners (assuming there are two), each of whom compares their new feelings

about the other person and about themselves to their memory of whatever special feelings now, in hindsight, they remember as inaugurating their love. Whether Obama (or any other president) loves a little boy

or a little girl is beside the point: what matters is the intensification of his love via the tender involuntary comparison with what it once was, so even if he someday thinks he's fallen out of love with his little girl or boy, that first moment of falling in love will nonetheless persist and

ruin everything for everyone. And so if I really want to live forever, to get worse continuously forever, I need to fall in love and stay there, because if love is comparative, it can only get better or worse, and it will always get worse. The crimes I've confessed to committing so far

aren't comparative in the same way: they don't refer back to an original crime. There is no first kiss of crime. It's true

that my crimes relate to each other, and new crimes revise the contexts of past crimes; they're a complex bundle of shitty acts and shitty memories which, like nerves, are extraordinarily

sensitive. But this bundle isn't bound by some original shitty act that englobes the later transgressions and governs everything I do. I didn't start committing more

crimes because I committed one crime: I had many reasons, too many to untangle. Love, on the other hand, cannot be balled up in the same way

because it rests on a single thing, even if that thing is impossible to capture: the moment of falling in love. This is why love is both a way out of the maze of crimes and an intensification

of those crimes: not only is love the worst, but it makes other awful things worse too: it interrupts the infinite oscillation between better and worse with sheer worsening: it gives me something great

to fail to live up to that has nothing to do with mother-father logic or the false enormity of the law, which, like

a saint, universalizes itself, say, in the body of a policeman killed in the line of duty by a gang member, like me, who fired seven times out of an ambiguous mixture of fear

and righteous anger: an unimportant episode, just one more brief entry in an almost never-ending list of things which are my fault. Crime is not enough, and now it never was.

So let's start with the love relationship. It's more than enough; it's too much, even. Say as a little boy I fall in love with a little girl. Even better, or much worse, say as an adult man I fall in love with an adult woman. It doesn't happen

in a glance, or even in a single passionate night, though a single passionate night is certainly a determining factor in the process, which is ongoing. Say a friend and I — a friend I've been wanting to sleep with but with whom the proper occasion has not arisen, because we're usually out with other friends

or alone together but busy pretending we're uninterested, which we do so well that we're each respectively convinced

that the other must not be that into it, though neither of us has completely ruled the possibility out either — go out for drinks. It's raining hard, but the weather's irrelevant. It's cold. We don't quite flirt. Instead, we rush a few cocktails and trade stories about our families. She tells me about her parents' divorce and I tell her what it's like to have parents who are still together. This discussion somehow avoids sliding into a different one about

love and sex, topics you bring up when you want the other person to start considering you in these terms. Eventually we walk back through the rain to my apartment and, after

a few more hours of conversation, have sex and fall asleep. The next morning we have sex again, twice. I think we both like it. But despite the seemingly

obvious enthusiasm we're showing for each other, a feeling of hesitant cloudiness hangs over us, not altogether unpleasant: there's no particular moment in which we know how to feel, nor a particular moment in which we feel like we need to know how we feel.

Over the next couple thousand years we've had sex countless times, but already in that first week

I dreamed about her, and, in the absence of an identifiably singular and pivotal moment of falling in love, I guess I'm positing

that dream as a kind of replacement for such a moment, at least in retrospect. My lover has freckled shoulders, which I like. Lots of freckles, which I like. They run down her arm and there's something about them that seems

soft to me, though of course there's no texture specific to freckles and they are not in and of themselves soft. I don't remember the dream, nor do I remember whether I remembered it when I woke.

Which reminds me of a dream I had when I was a little boy, about a little girl I had a crush on. Maybe it was my first crush, I don't know. But I've remembered the dream for thousands of years, and so it must be important, even if in some way I'll never be able to recognize. When I dreamed about this little girl, I imagined us

living together in an unreal and ideal space: I pictured our faces completely blank, voided of identifying features and wiped of expressive content, smiling just a little but not enough to make someone who saw us also smile, enlarged to the size of low grey

clouds, diffuse, hovering over the fuzzy image of a home — also relatively featureless, but more or less distinguishable as prototypically suburban and definitely armored in aluminum siding — in which, in this dream, we presumably

lived out, together, our blank and infinite lives. Some dreams don't require interpretation, and some do: family life is empty. Children know this. Their dreams of living out the empty lives proscribed to them are full of this knowledge. It's possible

that this will raise the hackles of certain family-oriented readers who feel that their domestic lives are meaningful and that no one, especially someone who hasn't known first hand

the joyful hard trials of motherhood/fatherhood, has the right to tell them otherwise, because after all

how can one person judge the intimacies of another and moreover it's just like an elitist New York snob to smear the good name of the Family, the common denominator of the world's everymen, the seat of exilic daily life and its creative

experiments with living well, that is, with making meaning out of a world in which there's none given, in which tedious jobs and sterile work-related friendships lock

people in their dumb houses to make of things what they can —
to make something of the love in the eyes of their sleepy husbands,
the tongue hanging out of the dog's mouth, the extra garlicky

biscuits that turned out to be a little too strong but were still pretty
good and you ate too many and now you're tossing and turning
trying to fall asleep with heartburn: no matter what you do, your
family life is stupid and meaningless and no one could possibly
care about it besides

the rest of your dipshit family and possibly your dipshit friends
who you see once every couple of weeks or so, if you're lucky,
because they're busy too, there's so much to do, it's hectic work
managing emptiness, the void could close up at any time and
you'd be left with the vague impression of something entirely
permanent, like endless suffering, or perpetual crime.

But it's not their fault. You can't blame those people who, bored to
death, hassled

to death, try their best in a bad situation, and it's not as if suffering
through cooking and cleaning and flipping channels and choosing
a new shade of beige paint together is inherently terrible — after
all, these activities are better

than the alternative, that is, cooking and cleaning and watching
television alone. But it's not no one's fault, either. It's someone's
fault: someone

bullied the whole world into neutered dyads and it wasn't someone
abstract and non-existent like Nature (who prefers lush prolifer-
ation) or Society (who prefers sterile isolation), or even, though I
would like to point a finger at it,

the English language, which deserves to be denounced for its role as an increasingly universal

flattener of meaning and crusher of spirits (even if it is a supposedly "living language" in terms of its colloquial plasticity and occasional expedience to literary artifice, it nonetheless most often functions as

a globalized technocratic code devoid of any arty bestial spontaneity or residual instinctive impulse to destruction), and which plays

a large part in the economic compartmentalization of feeling and the reduction of life to work insofar as its straightjacket phraseology

binds every attempt at an overflow of passionate verbosity to an ugly cascade of hackneyed cliché purified by decorative simile and a pervasive and predictable syllabic jangling, all rotten through by a more or less unstoppably nasal assonance

perfect only for the endlessly hee-hawing rhythms of market-speak and the contemplation thereof. It's not even good for

description, unless you want to describe the assholes who speak it, and the method of description is reduced, not even to naming, but to speaking in a way that performs

the thing described. And the worst part of all this is that the relative security of US family life (its banality disguised as good health — boredom as preventive medicine) justifies a world of horror:

this life and the means of saying it (that is, the shitty English language) have been elevated to an impossible ideal: people all over the world say they want to live like shit. They say this shitty life is better than any life that came before. It's not true. Life is miserable today for more people than it's ever been miserable for before (and not just because

there are more people on the planet): at least a quarter of the world lives in nearly complete immiseration and can barely feed themselves on what they make working sixteen hours a day in a sweatshop or an Apple factory or a lithium mine, and much of the other three quarters of the world population

aren't much better off, or are far better off but only financially and their lives are still miserable. Let's face it: life is worse now

than it's ever been. Only idiot liberals believe in unimpeded progress, while excusing today's plagues (which are killing millions of people denied access to patented pharmaceuticals), persecutions (in which

untold numbers of people have been slaughtered by guns and machetes and drones for their religious, ideological, or sexual practices, and sometimes even just because, for reasons that no one will ever untangle from the knots of government/corporate secrecy and/or the whims of territorial struggles), and slaveries (the extreme exploitation of human labor

in the global factory system) as bumps in a road that's already been paved, minor glitches

in a highly complex but functioning machine, like a spaceship. At least conservatives, if nothing else, are paranoid: they see decay everywhere they look, they see

the failure of women and men to love each other for all time and they even understand (in an obtuse way) that this inability to love is partly a side effect of the same economic mechanisms

which force people to waste their lives eating terrible food quickly so they can get back to their terrible jobs. To be sure, conservatives don't know what to make of it all, and their shitty

response is to fantasize about a better world before this one, a prelapsarian order that might be re-wrought by just the right iron

fist, by just the right murder of just the right immigrant. Of course there was no better world. Life has always been a dipshit. Even though the world we live in now is the worst one ever, there's no reason to think

that the previous worlds were any better. They were still bad. But at least those previous worlds, despite not being any better than this one when they existed, are a little bit

better now, because they no longer exist. Their atrocities are over, ours are ongoing. Sure, no one is writhing around in a bed of black plague, and no one is being tarred and feathered (or, if anyone is, probably only one or two people — if these things happen now it's not a *sign of the times* so much as a horrifying untimely aberration that reassures us about *how far we've come*), and that's good. But many people are starving

to death, in cities and slums, in public housing in the Bronx and improvised shacks in Jakarta; and many people are curled up in darkness in Bagram; and many people in the occupied Palestinian territories are being shot with DIME weapons which upon impact

release a burst of tungsten dust so that the projectile does not quite penetrate the body but the dust does, smothering the internal organs with poison metal; and many people in villages in Syria are shot in the road and left to rot; and many people are working multiple minimum wage jobs and will still be in debt for

their entire lives; and many people work in a couch cushion factory whose owners insist on using a certain hazardous glue because all the other couch cushion glues are supposedly too expensive and so most of the workers die of cancer at a relatively young age but

people have to work there anyway because there are no other jobs in that particular town and the populace has been forced into gratitude toward a company which treats their lives as expendable and meaningless even beyond the tedious hours

spent assembling couch cushions; and many people just die of loneliness; and many people are lonely for most of their lives and don't die of it, they just live that way; and many people are shot in the back

by police officers because they look suspicious; and many people are forced at automatic gunpoint into chipping away at tantalum by warlords who contract with Nintendo; and

many people are stolen into child slavery and sex slavery and often these kinds of slavery overlap; and many people are murdered all the time all over the world

for bending sexual norms even slightly in any direction; and Montsanto is killing all the bees. That's what's happening now. Plus a universe of simultaneous horrors too numerous to count but

hanging there like stars by which we decipher our location and beg guidance. Like the anarchic skyline of New York City, blinking

on and off and lighting up the whole sky. New York, after all, sucks the rest of the world into its orbit. It's the worst place on Earth. Partially because it's the center, and there's an intuitively logical way in which the center of something awful appears to be the worst and most abyssal part of that awful thing — for example, hell,

or the human heart. Much as the pomegranate stands in for the whole penis/vagina conundrum (but obviously more historically specific — because one can imagine the pomegranate's symbolic relation to genital pleasure

crossing historical boundaries, while a US city's role in global capitalism is limited to the time in which it played that role,

and the time in which the US, as a financial entity, even mattered to the rest of the world, that is, after its first revolution, in which righteous slaveholders who didn't want to pay taxes on their slaves fought for the right to buy more slaves, and before its banks

were burned to the ground — and geographical rather than biological, which makes it seem more impersonal, though of course

we all know how impersonal our bodies can be), New York has been symbolically fixed as the center of the world. All the world's horrors flow through it before arriving at their other destinations; every squeal of pain is muffled by the noise of its streets.

It all happens here. The rats drown. The buildings collapse. The men

who own everything dine. The men who own Germany dine. The men who own India dine. The men who own Saudi Arabia dine. The men who own Bank of America dine. The men who own Macy's dine. They all

dine. Sometimes they dine together. The people on their way to work hang their heads and avoid eye contact and every once in a while one of them throws up and the others huddle away. The jobs don't pay nearly enough to make up for whatever debt was incurred on the way to getting the job. The sky clouds over and it rains, just like everywhere else, except there's more pollution

in this sky than in most skies (except for those of cities where the environmental regulations are lax enough that US companies build factories there

to make products to sell to the people who live in New York) and the rain drags whatever's toxic in the air to the ground. The cars honk, always. There is usually

somebody screaming, either in pain or just because. The government records every cell phone call and archives them in some enormous secret archive. The police are required to go into poor Black neighborhoods

and pin people against walls and spread their legs and jam their hands into the pinned people's pockets and under their belts. The police are required

to shoot to kill. The food is mostly bad, but of course there are so many restaurants that some of them turn out to be pretty good. The expressway is loud and dirty and

rattles my apartment constantly. My room

is small. It's incredibly humid in the summer. The balding men who work in the financial district

are very poorly dressed, even though their clothes are more expensive than my small room; they look like

leaky grey balloons. The women in bars get drunk enough to sleep with these men, seemingly on purpose. The commercial centers are so crowded that people faint. There's a video of a man on the subway

licking his shoe. Much of the best graffiti has been sandblasted.
Brooklyn is crawling with white devils. The elderly die of
dehydration

in the heat and freeze to death in the cold. Public housing is
infested with roaches, bed bugs, and rats. It's raining. The UN is
here. The police seem

to be everywhere at once; the city is overrun with their little
walkie-talkies. The mayor is a billionaire of dicks bent on

reigning in violence in poor neighborhoods by arresting and
imprisoning more of their residents, often for possessing

small amounts of drugs or for "resisting arrest." He has thirty-three
billion dicks. The only reason New York has become so *nice*

is the intensification of police violence against its poor and Black
and Latino populations. Plus the simultaneous relaxation of
financial regulations which has dragged

the median income of those with already high median incomes so
much higher that now they can just buy up every old building and
tear it down and build shitty new buildings

with those enormous windows that rich people seem to like
because the rest of us can see their big black leather couches and
stupid antique lamps. There are surveillance cameras on every
block. Sexual assault is so common that women

expect a certain amount of harassment on the street. The new
stadium is really ugly. The bicycle lanes are too narrow and
bicyclists are frequently hit by car doors.

But the worst thing about all this is that the people who live here

somehow convince themselves that this city is better than other cities because you can see blue-chip art anytime you want and homeless people are kicked out of the parks. (Similarly, the

worst thing about our historical moment is that we've convinced ourselves it's somehow

better than other times, because of frozen food and antibiotics.) And since New York City is the worst place ever, I might as well make it worse, because

it's not going to get any better and even if it did it would only get worse at the same time: for example, if the housing authority were to scrub the black mold from all of their buildings, then those buildings might fetch

a higher price when the housing authority is subsequently disman-tled and its properties are

sold to developers who turn them into luxury apartments. Even worse, because New York is the symbolic center of the world, when bad things happen elsewhere (as they constantly do), it's still

to blame. When the Taliban bombs a voting booth: New York money. When a fabric factory collapses in Bangladesh: New York money. When the seas are emptied of tuna: New York money. And so on. It's not even controversial or especially interesting

to point out that the US, and especially New York, finances

the world's endless atrocities. It's simply the case, without much room for interpretation or debate, except of course

for interpretation and debate about exactly what circuitous or direct path a certain amount of New York money has

taken on its way to paying for the bullet which ripped off part of
a Somali woman's foot or the mile-wide tornado which just tore
through Oklahoma. It's all here. And so

I did it here. I had to do it here. There's no other place to do it.
Even if I tried to do it somewhere else it wouldn't work, not in the
sense that it wouldn't happen, because it would certainly happen,
it already happened, but it wouldn't stay there, it would shift its
burden of responsibility

somewhere else, not only out of my hands but out of my sight too,
so that I wouldn't be able to see who did it, or who was supposed
to have done it, that is, me, and so definitely couldn't blame
myself, which I should, because I deserve to be blamed, because I
did it, and as long

as I did it here, which I did, then even if I didn't do it, which I
did, I'm still embedded in the city's guilt, not in the sense of its
conscience — it has no conscience, it's a city — but in the sense of
its literal

centrality with regards to death and destruction, and as long as
I'm in it I'm central too, I function catachrestically as a piece of
the city — like a side street, or a basement apartment, or a broken
water main — and since New York is the best

place in the worst world because at least it continually works to
destroy that world, to make it even worse, then I can also be, for a
time, the best, by doing

all the major and minor terrible things I can, and getting away
with it, as every piece of the city — like a park bench, or a
Dunkin' Donuts drive-through, or a weird look on a friend's

face — gets away with all the major and minor horrible things it does, murder and worse, dropping white phosphorus on civilian populations and burning most of their skin off,

for example. So say I was driving from my apartment in Crown Heights to a friend's house in Ditmas. It's not a long trip, but just long enough to drift

a little, to space out and play a game with yourself in which you try to remember

the kinds of things that are usually hard to remember but occasionally just set themselves up in your thoughts, like the shape of your dad's haircut on the back of his neck or the feeling of

reading. So say I was driving but not really paying attention when

I slammed on the brakes. I didn't know why. I just did it, out of some deep or shallow instinctive or perceptive notion or impulse, those obscure layers of the organism that order you around and force you

to slam on the brakes when you weren't planning on it, among other quasi-involuntary things; that is, the slamming was basically out

of my control and yet could in no way be mistaken for anything other than something I did. I might have stopped the car, but I didn't mean to, and I certainly didn't mean to run anyone over. His legs

were bent like pieces of art behind his back. There was blood everywhere (although I might be exaggerating), and I thought I saw some body parts dangling from trees. Once again without knowing quite what I was doing but doing it anyway, I slammed on the gas but missed the pedal and scraped the side of my ankle so that the car lurched

forward and came to rest with one wheel on some small part of the crushed-up man I hit, probably just an arm. I tried again and drove away. When I pulled up to my friend's apartment building, I sat in the car for a while.

(He has a roach problem, but it's relatively under control, not nearly as bad as many of the roach-related horror stories one hears about in New York. For example, my girlfriend

told me about an apartment where she used to live in which the roaches were so abundant that if you turned on

the kitchen light after dark, they would be blanketing the walls; even worse, she said, they lived in the microwave, and you could see their silhouettes

crawling across the back side of the LED clock. If you shook this microwave, she said, out of curiosity or because you might have thought that shaking it was somehow equivalent to cleaning it, dozens of roaches would pour out and scurry into the walls, which, by the way, were covered with black mold,

as they are in many New York apartments, some of which are so dramatically filthy

that the idea of apartment hunting is overwhelming and it seems easier to just stay where you are, even if your current apartment

is cramped or on an inconvenient train line, because if it doesn't have too much of a roach or mold problem, or bedbugs, it

seems reasonable to be grateful for what you have and plant your-self there for as long as you can, though this gratitude is frustrating

because when you feel required to feel grateful you end up hating
the thing you are supposed to be grateful for. Like when you go to
a party at a rich old couple's enormous house and you're expected
to be completely bowled over

by their generosity — a gratitude you would never be required
to feel if you were visiting anyone who wasn't rich — and you're
supposed to be impressed

and thankful for the chance to bask in the aura of what their
collection of objects represent: a careless

flow of money that can be spent on clothes so expensive they don't
need to fit, which I admittedly like, and cars with doors that open
from the roof, which I think are dumb, and basically anything else
that can be bought — but all you can bring yourself to feel is hate
[admittedly mixed with envy, which intensifies the hate and turns
it against yourself, which you know

is what *they* want you to feel, which makes you hate them more]
until later on that night when you're lying in your cramped room
overhot and

half-asleep and floating in and out of another one of those violent
dreams you don't want to sink completely into because you know
you'll wake up

tense if you do, and so you're keeping your eyes partly open, trying
not to fall asleep quite yet, when the sound of a woman shrieking

startles you and you stick your face into the window's dirty screen
and try to peer out, vaguely wondering if you should call 911 but
unable to spatialize

the scream, it sounds like it's coming from all directions at once,
and so what can you do, call up the police and say, *I hear a scream*

somewhere and it sounds like someone is in pain? So you lay back down instead,

head buried in your pillow, listening intently but trying not to listen, and you fall asleep much faster than you would expect.)

I sat and listened to the inside of the car as if I'd be able to hear something in it, something voiceless in the quiet which might speak about what happened, which might confess to its involvement

in the fatal hit-and-run that just took a teenager's life; but of course I heard nothing, there was nothing to hear. I cursorily inspected the front of the car (the hood was dented but that's nothing, many hoods are dented) and rang the bell.

It was always nice to see this friend. He had just gotten a new tattoo and was eager to show it off. It was on his chest, a few inches above the nipple, and said, in an elaborate cursive that struck me as overdoing it a little, "Fuck Yes." I said I liked it, though I didn't know if I really did, or

if I really didn't for that matter, because I was busy thinking about whether or not I would get a tattoo like that, which I definitely wouldn't. We opened

a few beers and stood around chatting in his kitchen. (I didn't see any roaches that night. In fact, I never actually saw roaches in his apartment, I only heard

about them.) I asked him what his girlfriend thought of his new tattoo. He said at first she

wasn't exactly thrilled with the idea but then she got used to it. But does she like it, or is she just "used to it?" I asked. Well, he said, it took some convincing. It's not that she was against the idea of a tattoo per se, but that this particular tattoo

seemed kind of stupid to her. I explained that it's something I've wanted since I was in college, but that only proved her point. What point? I asked. I was asking needling questions, because the tattoo seemed like a funny

decision to me, and I wanted to understand it. Well, he said, I'm not sure, I guess, but something about

the whole thing being kind of childish, I think. Do you think she thinks

all tattoos are childish, or just that this tattoo is particularly childish? I asked. I guess it probably is particularly childish, but I didn't mean for it to be childish, he said. Haha, I said. Haha,

he replied. Someday, I said, you'll be a dad with a "Fuck Yes" tattoo over your nipple. You'll be a dad on the beach

playing in the sand with your kids. And you'll have a "Fuck Yes" tattoo over your nipple. Haha, he said. Haha, I replied. Well, I think of it more as a way to mark time, he said. Do you think you've come

to some sort of turning point? I asked. No, not necessarily, he said. So what kind of time are you marking? I asked. Well, it's not like all important moments in somebody's life are turning points, he said. I guess

so, I said. I mean, sometimes you feel like you've reached a place in your life that you feel good about, he said. Like you've come to a plateau? I asked. Haha, not at all, he said, I just keep getting better, haha, no, but I've come to a place I feel good about. Well, what I don't understand, I guess, I said, is how

you can mark time and not have it become a turning point. What do you mean? he asked. I mean, I said, well, as soon as you mark time, even if you're not trying to mark a specific time, doesn't it become a turning point? Because you'll always look back on it and say, oh,

that's when I marked that time, and then you'll measure other things, later life events or whatever, from there. I get what you mean, he said, but that's

not what I'm talking about. (This is what our conversations were like, because it's hard for men to relate to each other, or to anyone.) My friend offered me another beer and I took it. Then I realized

we hadn't clinked bottles so I extended my bottle

and he extended his and we both said, Cheers. Well, he asked, did you go to that reading by that poet that neither of us likes the other night? No, I said, I didn't go, did you? No, he said, I didn't go either. Yeah, I said, it didn't seem like there was any reason

to go except to hate it. Yeah, he said, that poet that neither of us likes is such a bad poet. Yeah, I said, I don't know why people like that writing so much, since it's so bad. Yeah, he said. Really bad. Well,

he said, I'm looking forward to that poet who we both like a little bit's reading next week. Oh yeah, that should be good, I said. It should be OK, he said. Yeah, it'll be OK, I said. Oh I forgot to tell you, he said, I heard something funny about that poet who we both like a little bit, but I guess I don't know if it's true. Oh, I said, tell me. Well, I actually don't know anything, he said, but I heard that this other

poet whose work we don't know but who we've met occasionally at parties told a poet who

we actually like that they know something so bad about the poet who we both like a little bit that they can never tell anyone what it is. I really want to know what it is, I said. Me too, he said. Who do you think

will tell us? I asked. Well, it seems like this other poet whose work we don't know but who we've met occasionally at parties is the only person

who knows, or at least they're only person that we know knows, and I don't know that poet well enough to ask, he said. Yeah, I said, I don't know that poet well enough either. Or at all, really. I've only met that poet at parties. Me too, he said, I guess we'll never know. Yeah, we'll

never know, I said. Yeah, he said. We opened more beers. I leaned against the kitchen counter and absentmindedly fiddled with the knobs on the stove, twisting them

on just enough to hear a little gas hiss out, and then flicking them back off. My friend noticed this but didn't say anything. I couldn't smell the gas, which mildly surprised me. I tried sniffing

deeply without being obvious about it. There was a cool dampness in the air I hadn't noticed before. What's the worst place

you've ever lived? he asked. You mean the worst apartment or the worst city? I asked. Oh, good point, he said, I guess either one. Hm, I said, well, I haven't lived anywhere awful, but there was one place that was pretty dirty. Dirty

because you never cleaned it, or just dirty? he asked. Oh, just dirty, I said. It came dirty, and it stayed that way. But it really wasn't so bad. I guess I've lived

in more or less decent places, most of the time. What about you? Well, he said, my last apartment was very small, and there were those stains in the shower that looked like blood stains. I remember that, I said. But overall that wasn't so bad, he said, even though

it was expensive and small. But oh, there was one place that I never lived in,

he said, that was worse, in a way. Me and my girlfriend at the time signed the lease and everything, we were all ready to move in, and then I freaked out

because it was on the first floor and there were no bars on the window, so we broke the lease and never moved in. Haha, I said, really? Yeah, really, he said, I can't handle the first floor. I have a real fear of home invasion. Haha, why? I asked. What

do you mean, why? he asked. It's horrifying. Imagine you're asleep

and someone is standing over your bed, watching you. And you don't even know it, I said. Exactly, he said, and you don't even know it. And the worst part is that there are basically only two things that could happen: either the person standing over you and watching you just

punches you in the face, or dumps a pot of boiling water on your bed, or stabs you, or otherwise inflicts permanent bodily injury before you even have a chance to beg him or her not to do it, or they don't do anything, they just watch you for awhile, maybe all night, they just stand there looking at you and when you wake up you never know it happened. In some ways, that sounds even worse. What if someone watched

you every night without you knowing it? he asked. Haha, I said. (Once I had a mildly erotic dream about this

friend, in which I sat next to him at a dinner table and covertly reached under the long tablecloth to caress

his smooth and womanly legs.) What if they also left something behind, so that you knew someone was there but you never knew who they were or why they broke in? I asked. Like

what? he asked. Like a chain, I said. A chain? he asked. Yeah, I said, they just leave a chain somewhere in the house so when you wake up you find a chain. But why would they do that? he asked. So that you would know

they'd been there, I said. Haha, he said. See, that's what I mean, he said. It's a horrifying thought. And I couldn't live with that, I couldn't

worry about that every night before I fell asleep, wondering if it would finally happen, or if I would wake up tied to the bed. I didn't know

what to say, so I asked for a glass of water. My friend poured me one and handed me another beer. For a while I alternated

between the glass of water and the bottle of beer, sipping from one and fingering the other, fidgeting without

really noticing it. And because my friend didn't seem to notice my fidgeting either, I assumed that I did it all the time. I'm always fidgeting: screwing the caps on and off bottles, picking at my cuticles until they bleed, pulling at the short hairs of my beard, rubbing my nose, rubbing my eyes, digging wax out of my ears, scraping the plaque from my teeth,

massaging my neck, ruffling my hair or neatening the part, straightening

a curl between two fingers and letting it go so that it curls again, tapping my skull, palming my knees, tugging at my socks. And so on. I'm always moving. I can't stop moving. It's not even that I assume

I'm always moving in a particular way, recognizable as an idiosyncratic quirk that can be tolerated or eventually, with familiarity, ignored; rather, I assume I'm always moving so erratically

that my friends can't or don't bother to identify any particular repetitive movement with my personality, but see me as a jittery accretion of twitches: little residual imitations of body language and nervous energy. (You see, I'm all kinds of men:

the kind of man who holds his head to one side when someone else is speaking; the kind of man who keeps his head straight when listening to someone else's argument, as if the effort

of holding it up were a minor distraction he needs to help him concentrate; the kind of man who tilts his head back a little when someone else laughs; the kind of man who

waits for someone else to smile and then abruptly laughs in preemptive affirmation of their good humor; the kind of man who shakes his head and smiles

instead of laughing when he can't muster an actual laugh, either

because he doesn't find the supposedly funny thing funny or
because he truly does find the supposedly funny thing funny

but the pressure to laugh when everyone else is laughing is stifling;
the kind of man who shakes his head while laughing as if to

reassure whoever's with him that he doesn't take his own laughter
seriously, that his mind is on more serious considerations

and that the present conversation is merely an entertaining stopgap
between solitary bouts of brooding reflection; the kind of man
who nods both when he agrees and

when he doesn't; the kind of man who looks someone else in the
eyes when they say something

stupid but refuses to argue or rant; the kind of man who stretches
his neck

out when someone corrects him; the kind of man who looks away
when someone else looks away, and looks back when he thinks
they're looking back, and looks away again

if they're still looking away; the kind of man who stares at his
fingernails; the kind of man who doesn't shake his head yes or no
so much as jerk it indiscernibly, so that whoever

he's conversing with repeats their question or opinion, thinking
that the jerking simply implied that the other person (that's me)
didn't hear or understand, and only when he (me again) jerks it
again

does the other person (not me) understand that the person he or
she is talking to just does that, jerks his head to signify yes or no,
and yet it isn't clear why he does that,

it doesn't necessarily evoke either a positive or a negative response so much as the choice between a positive or negative response, and this choice is finally made only when I just answer the question already

because the person I'm talking to can't seem to read my body language, which I think is perfectly intelligible and moreover more subtle and expressive than my spoken affirmations, which suffer from a stiff quaver that strongly implies I might not quite mean what I say; the kind of man who bites his nails even when he's not nervous; the kind of man who tears

the dead skin from his cuticles with his teeth; the kind of man who sticks the tip of his tongue out between his lips

when he's absentminded; the kind of man who puffs his cheeks

in the middle of a conversation, which he believes, for some reason, makes it look like he's paying close attention or contemplating something someone else just

said; the kind of man who exhales loudly when exasperated or bored; the kind of man who makes a fist and blows into it even when he's not cold, for the pleasure of warm air on his palm, and to do something mechanical and repetitive

while conversing or reading aloud; the kind of man who occasionally

just looks at his palms and studies the lines and wrinkles as if he would be able to tell if they were getting deeper; the kind of man who, when he's biting his fingernails, licks

them and examines the way they shine, turning his hand in the light; the kind of man who squints after someone else makes a point that he considers a main point; the kind of man who thinks he's holding his head at a casual slant but looks to others as if he's in pain; the kind of man who does neck and back exercises in public places and even occasionally when he's in the middle

of saying something, so that the exercises seem almost like emphasis; the kind of man who blinks suspiciously; the kind of

man who moans whenever something aches, like his head or his feet, but doesn't think he's moaning in order

to attract the attention of whoever hears him moan — he thinks the sound is spontaneous and wholly personal, directed toward his own small relief at hearing his discomfort vocalized; the kind of man who, when sitting next to a sunny window, holds his head in the hot glare past the point

of comfort and even after it starts to hurt because he enjoys ducking back into a bit of shade and feeling the cool delicate sensitivity returning to his cheeks; the kind of man who looks directly at your head

when you talk, as if considering whether your eyes would be open or closed if it were detached from your body; the kind of man who takes deep breaths

too frequently when he's listening to you, like every thirty seconds; the kind of man who smiles and laughs silently whenever he agrees with something instead of risking a justification of his agreement with an augmentary fact or viewpoint, which is harder to take back.)

Eventually I left. By then my friend and I were lightly drunk, and our conversation had devolved into the sort of minor complaints (about our jobs, acquaintances, finances, etc) that impose themselves on a conversation when friends have nothing left to say to each other, out of exhaustion or insobriety or encroaching boredom. Hug? he asked. We

hugged goodbye. I slouched to my car and drove safely home.

Ten years later, my girlfriend and I were fighting about directions. I don't remember the details of the argument, what the streets were named or even what town

we were passing through, I only remember the style. She was doing that thing where she subordinates

the expression of a diffusive bitterness (a feeling not unlike the sensation of

heat or cold, especially intense in certain sensitive spots but not limited to those spots alone) to the stress of a present-tense banality, so that the by-definition extreme triviality of the banal tableaux is elevated

to the level of a cause: as if the familiar everydayness of an ostensibly minor discord (for example, a wrong turn or an overlong silence) were the source of a deep-seated, almost abdominal, pride of resentment. I was doing that thing

where I offer only slight nods in her direction and feign an exaggerated attentiveness to the road (looking straight ahead can be searing), adding to the empty tension

piling up between us. I hid my free hand in my lap. She did the same with hers, so that either of us would have had to reach

across the entire front seat to grasp the other's hand and sweetly knead its fingers between our own, as a sort of tacit request for a mutual de-escalation of nervousness, which we both knew was not going to happen. This was a shitty thing to do, and I knew it, and even worse I didn't even want

her to feel ignored (the aim of my silence was not particularly precise or self-assured), I just wanted her to know that I was mostly conscious of doing something shitty, and that my shittiness was an intended effect,

not a residual symptom of unprocessed anger or an ill-timed absentmindedness: I wanted her to see right through me, to know that I was feigning a flat blank silence

to make her mad at me, and not just because I was mad myself (in fact, I wasn't actually mad, I was just feeling mean). In turn, she was doing that thing where she acknowledges my meanness by rolling her eyes (a gesture

which in my girlfriend's case connotes disappointment more than irritation, or perhaps I experience her irritation as disappointment, in her or in me I can't tell) and decides to wait it out, as if

in a few minutes, or, at most, hours, I'll give up

this stupid game and pretend that I was never playing it, which I will; and though it's possible that her eye-rolling was also meant to inflame my anger and curl me out of silence, because she knew that any response at all would have probably

deflated the particular kind of sloppy male meanness I was going for, I took it to be a signal of her temporary resignation, a version of a sigh, which left me alone with my own dumb thoughts, and so we both sat there silently for a long while

while I scolded myself for ever having played non-responsive in the first place, because it would have been comforting to talk about anything, even about my non-responsiveness and why I wield it like a weapon and what I think it's supposed to accomplish, which was not a topic

that I wanted to explore in depth, because that sort of reproachful self-examination, when facilitated by a lover, makes me feel like I'm on trial, though I've never been,

and the shriveling up that I tend to do when I feel like I'm trapped in my own personal version of being on trial is literalized on my face as a sort of old man grimace, an almost involuntary neuronal pinching that some dipshit therapist might term "counterproduc-tive" insofar as it serves

to cut me emotionally off from my girlfriend, who is, after all, only trying to learn more about me and the grammar of my happiness, because she ostensibly cares and wants to help manage said happiness,

though we all know what happens if you try to manage happiness, the same thing that happens if you try to manage grammar. I guess I made a wrong turn. I guess I said something I shouldn't have

said. I guess I should have smiled even if I didn't want to smile. And I guess my girlfriend should have just borne it patiently and silently when I decided to

pretend that I wasn't listening to her. I guess she should have planned on conforming to whatever ironic mood I felt like indulging. I guess she didn't say what I wanted her to say when I expected her to know what I wanted her to say. That's what's

so bad about love, I think: it's all guessing, all the time. Unlike talking with a friend, talking with a lover involves persistently guessing what they'll think in response to whatever you say, and comparing that to what you think you meant to say, which, of course, was always

better than what they think you said, which was somehow mutilated in the saying, and came out hurtful; a friend, on the other hand, accepts everything you say as it is, which is not to say that

a friend doesn't misread you or take things overly personally or twist your words, but only that you're not necessarily reduced to guessing

how badly they're hurt or how deeply they will now resent you forever. In fact, when a friend misunderstands you, it's often simple enough to laugh it off as a sign of intimacy, a reminder of the differences that

ground your mutual appreciation (of course there are all sorts of psychic struggles played out between you — for example, aspects of what seems like one person's personality snaking around within the other person and one or the other, probably both, parties

occasionally resenting the friendship's intrusion into their so-called private thoughts — but these struggles don't come to define you

in quite the same way as the struggle of love does, unless the friendship is also a love relationship, which it often is) and the sexual tension that sustains it. But everybody knows

that you can't say the right thing to a lover. It will never happen. It's impossible. One

meaning of love, assuming it has any, is perpetual misprision and its attendant creative hurt. And this hurt can be exploited by someone who wishes, consciously or not, to be worse, which, lucky for me,

I do. So I do that. In fact, I do it all the time. I did it many times before my episode of embittered righteous silent driving, and I did it later too, say a hundred years later, when the world had changed dramatically but I was still

misunderstanding my girlfriend, purposefully pretending

to be wounded by her pained incomprehension of something I said which she knew was meant to hurt her, but which for some reason I insisted

hurt me, insofar as she misunderstood it, thus forcing a corresponding feeling of estrangement on both of us, right in the middle of a perfectly nice summer morning when the day feels open and free, why does she have to ruin everything, why do I. The world is worse than ever, it remains

the worst. The only thing it really does is get worse. A hundred years after my girlfriend and I fell in love, people still worked

terrible jobs: moving boxes, putting boxes together, taking boxes apart, recycling boxes, burning

fields of Indian wheat, slaughtering enormous genetically-modified chickens with enormous mechanical blades, supervising the last desperate mining of the nearly empty Afghani lithium fields, picking toxic trash out of the trickling waterways, lifting heavy boxes

filled with toxic and/or non-toxic trash and packing them into aluminum pods, thumbing data onto a dock, driving the pods to the docks, hauling concrete across a room, dropping white phosphorus on the shores of Somalia, guarding the international prison in Iceland, chipping at rocks with a file, shucking corn, harvesting the jellyfields,

screwing caps onto a thousand bottles a day, testing a thousand light switches a day, pushing bodies into graves, running experiments on cosmic minerals, purifying water, carrying handfuls of pebbles from one end of a construction site

to the other, disseminating false information in Caracas Buenos Aires Rio Lima and Havana, planting small explosive devices in Hong Kong Sydney St. Petersburg Damascus Lagos and Mumbai, hammering nails into

beams, repairing Baskets, affixing labels to a thousand cans of tuna a day, pouring pills into a thousand pill bottles a day, measuring a thousand nozzles a day, driving a garbage

truck, being a cop. Jobs were like everything else: they got worse. Employers still paid people to do the evil shit that they would never stoop to doing, and the rest of us were still stuck

with gratitude for the opportunity to wish these wasted hours of our lives were over. And our lives grew

longer. We had more time to work more jobs. I worked all those jobs. I had so much time to hate. I hated. One day — and there were many days like this — my girlfriend and I were riding our scooters to work, side by side, and because we were too tired to converse at length, we tried

striking up a roughly commute-length conversation about our jobs. This was a bad idea. Almost immediately I felt like she was trying to say something about me by way of her complaints about her boss. For instance, her boss doesn't allow his employees to use their Baskets while Jumping, which I completely agree is a needlessly punitive prohibition, but when she brings it up I take it as a comment on my dislike

of after-work Basket-play, which I keep insisting has nothing to do with a moralizing judgment on anyone's form of decompressive downtime, and I understand perfectly

well that people need to relax and spin a Basket or two after a long day of work, especially if they Jump all day, but because my own job requires me to be spinning Baskets for hours at a time I just don't have any desire to come home and get right back to it, but really how can I convince you that

this is not some kind of judgment or passive-aggressive commentary on what you perceive to be my idea of your laziness, it's how I feel. And of course she must know that by bringing up her boss's admittedly old-fashioned aversion to on-the-clock Basket-play, she's implicating

me in his corny old-fashionedness, which to some degree I admittedly embrace, but which is also something that I don't particularly like about myself, especially

considering that it drives a wedge between us and results in the kind of petty bickering in which one person (in this case my girlfriend) puts on saintly airs simply because they do what everyone else does and in so doing destroys

some solipsistic part of themselves, and the other person (in this case me) puts on the airs of a snobby bitch who can't stomach the simple inescapable giant human fact of enduring commonalities with others (especially banal commonalities such as shared entertainments, which upset one's lofty contrarian expectations of oneself) and so acts as if

he has none, which performance, of course, anybody can and does see through immediately — it's a common enough act, you see it all the time. And so when my girlfriend talked about her boss I clammed up. I knew she was talking about me, and

I, out of spite, obdurately decided to extend the conversation (we had a relatively long ride to work, after all, and nothing is worse for a couple attempting to rekindle an incremental closeness than a long ride in meaningfully dead silence) by

apologizing or explaining away my inability to extend the conversation in a more genuine and/or patronizing fashion, so I said I was sorry

and that I was tired, I wasn't keeping quiet out of spite or because I was harboring secret resentful thoughts but just because it was early and I didn't sleep well and I was exhausted

in advance of the long day ahead of me, which is probably the more or less timeless way people in committed relationships have of simultaneously opening up and closing down discussion, because they want to say something but can't think of anything

that's not shitty so say, but it was also true, I was tired and I did have a long day ahead of me. For good reason, she understood

this half-hearted test of conciliation as a passive-aggressive attempt to undermine the severity of her own long day ahead of her, as if she didn't have to work at least as hard as I did or was not as committed

to being completely exhausted by the repetitive stupidity of her work, which was true, not that she didn't work as hard as I did, which she probably did and I knew that, but that I wanted to suggest that she didn't, I think, and my self-deluded whimpering about how tired I was was

certainly not simply meant to fill up conversational space or even to amplify the awkwardness between us (because everyone knows

that following an awkward pause with news of your supposed tiredness or absentmindedness is just a means of elongating that pause) but also to make her feel guilty for

not being as tired as me, or not leaving the idea of the two of us alone when it was perfectly apparent to us both that there wasn't going to be, not right now, a

short stretch of quality time or casual intimacy with which we could, respectively, relieve in domestic fantasy the loneliness of our long work days, and which might give us reason to wait for the inevitable slow arrival

of some sort of evening together. And then I was the one scrambling for something to say, after I had said the stupidest thing I could have said short of saying something offensive or confrontational, and my lover

rode on next to me in silence, refusing to acknowledge either my existence or the shittiness of the needling thing I said with

a reproach, which would have at least been mercifully to-the-point, as it were, that is, to any point at all, which could then be used, by one or the other of us, to make another point, which accumulation of points might eventually add up to an actual conversation. We met for lunch later that

afternoon and didn't say much then either. This went on, and it didn't. We didn't talk, and then we talked, and then we didn't talk again. Hundreds of years passed, and through them all

the world remained the worst, while our love only got worse, and stronger. Those were great days, in the sense that they felt big and historic. Somewhere in there

were 70 years or so of relatively egalitarian peace, after the US was abolished but before Obama returned to power and flooded Hungary with trillions of gallons of fake water, which sparked

the global air crisis that led to a series of not so much wars as vicious retaliatory ankle biting: one country (or fragment of

a country) would fling chemical weapons into another, and then that one would use a heat ray on the capital of yet another country, melting the eyes

out of their leaders' heads, and that country, in a predictably . chaotic and leaderless frenzy, would lash out with their most brutal but not necessarily most effective

military inventions, firing digital spikes into their neighbor's food supply, or burning their seeds, or darkening

their skies with a heavy black smoke that hung low for months and squeezed the life out of flowers, and so on. But eventually, a thousand years from when we fell in love, when there was no more

US (divvied up) or New York City (underwater) and the English language had been significantly altered by the infiltration of the monocode, there just weren't that many humans left

to fight with each other, or to police national borders. By then I had treated my lover awfully

for a long time, and she had treated me awfully, and we were

happier than we'd ever been. We occasionally — every couple
dozen years or so, enough time to convincingly repeat the
heartbreaking surprise

of seeing a certain potential for violence in a person whom you had
previously felt protected by — beat each other, or rather one of us

beat the other, and occasionally the police were called and
someone was briefly locked

up, when there were still police, in the old sense. But we also
fucked every day, for a thousand years, and sometimes a couple

times a day: and I never slept with anyone else (or, rather, when I
did sleep with someone else I told her about it — begged forgive-
ness, demanded assuagement), though I was sometimes careful

to imply that I was carrying on a few secret affairs, because actu-
ally secretly sleeping with someone else would inspire forgiveness,
which I already had more than enough of, and it's much worse to
stay faithful when your lover suspects or

feels certain of your unfaithfulness, and accepts it without discus-
sion, because she worries that an accusation would both anger

me and bring to the surface painful details that are better off
submerged, left to rust at the bottom of the sea, and after all I
probably don't even remember

those women, they're probably dead by now, and even if they aren't
they must be absolutely elderly, probably skeletal, and well past the
rosy-cheeked

age at which they were threats to our constancy, except for the most
recent women whom my girlfriend thinks I slept with, who are

of course (she imagines) young and beautiful but also predictably immature and needy, and she knows I wouldn't put up with

that kind of post-adolescent psychodrama for long enough to shake the compulsory security and emotional distance that sustains a love as old and bad as ours. Love lasts

too long. We tried many things to interrupt it,

though never enough. She would suck my cock while I slapped her pussy. I would lick her pussy while she pulled my hair. I would pull her hair

while she just lay there. She would finger herself while looking at me, and I would stick a hairbrush-handle-shaped object up my ass while I watched her

watch me, and I wouldn't even touch my cock, I would just let it bounce a little and moan. She would

lie on her back and lift her spread legs into the air while I lay diagonally over her and we would kiss deeply but not quite hard, and I would hold my open mouth just a few centimeters

above hers so she could thrust her tongue up between my teeth and I could dribble saliva down over it and all down her chin and neck, and even though her pussy and asshole were

bared just for me, wide open and waiting to be pinched with clothespins or paperclips, I wouldn't see them, my eyes would be closed and I'd painfully withhold concentration on everything but the wetness

of her lips as they brushed mine and the flatness of her breasts as they were crushed to the weight of my chest. Once I invited my friend over and asked her to suck one of his cocks while I sucked the other; his tattoo

had faded by then, he was an old man, and I got off on her feigned repulsion, or perhaps she was truly repulsed

by the texture of his hard rubbery cocks, or perhaps she was turned on but part of that specific feeling of being turned on

involved pretending to be turned off, I couldn't tell and she wouldn't tell me. Or she would stick her whole hand up her pussy and pull out

a bloody hand — she had torn herself — and I would smell it while I jerked off. Or I would stick my cock between her toes (to the best of my ability) and fuck her foot. Or I would spread her asshole as wide as I could with whatever wide thing

I could find while she begged me not to or begged me to keep going, out of embarrassment or pride. Or she would beg

me to touch her while I pretended to ignore her pleas and read news on the internet. Or I would hold her down

and run my tongue over every ticklish part of her body while she squirmed and giggled and promised that she loved me. And at least once she

tied me to the bed and sat on my face so that I was suffocating and my muffled cries for air and mercy vibrated through her clit, and she grabbed a handful of my hair and pulled my head

harder into her slick hairy pussy while squatting her weight down into my mouth like she was force-feeding me, and my cries grew simultaneously louder with desperation and more muffled as if screamed softly from far away, say by someone on the other side of a prison wall having his fingernails torn off or

in the hallucinatory throes of a hunger strike. Or she would fuck my mouth with her fingers until her entire hand

was dripping with spit, and then she would lick off and swallow as much of it as she could. This is hardly everything we did. We did

much more. Though of course we didn't try all sexual positions, practices, or combinations, simply because there are some we never got around to, not yet, given that there are literally an infinite

number of ways of having sex. And if other people are involved, which they sometimes were, the possibilities quickly and exponentially multiply, especially since my girlfriend prefers women, and they

can be pretty inventive. On our own, we occasionally reached limits (for example, we did some slapping and biting and whipping, but we

never got as far as, say, stabbing or cutting, probably simply because of the banal bourgeois cowardice at the heart of my — and eventually possibly our — wish to be worse), but the presence of others pushed us to new pleasures, even though they could never be, despite

their novelty, enough for us: no matter how many asses we reddened with the palms of our hands or

bruised with belts, it wouldn't be enough, we would never get to the bottom of those asses, to the end of the feeling of fraudulence that pervades the entire human body and especially the eyes. But still, after a thousand years of energetic fucking and talking and loving each other miserably, some things change, and new possibilities arise precisely where they had previously been unthinkable. And so when

we reached the point, about two thousand years after we got together, when we didn't need our voices anymore, at least not here in the Three Wealthy Countries, I reversed

my previous opinion on self-mutilation. As you know, the intro-duction of speech-console implants meant that the monocode could be vocalized digitally, and you didn't need

to learn it, in the old sense; nobody misspoke, and communication was effectively perfected. It no longer seemed like such a bad idea to cut out my tongue, which meant that it was now a worse thing to do than it used to

be. But my lover still wouldn't like it, not at all. Like everyone else who has a body, I've always hated mine. It's a fake. A total fucking fake. I don't piss like that. I don't

snore like that. I don't fart like that. My armpits don't flake and itch like that. My lips don't blister. I don't let out a mangled little scream when I sneeze. I don't compulsively pick

at the fungus on my toenails like that. My teeth don't stink when they rot. My back doesn't sweat through every shirt I own in the scorching summer years and sometimes through two or three shirts a day. I don't say things I don't mean. I don't bruise so easily. I don't suffer

painful rashes on my thighs. My girlfriend, of course, has a different relationship to my body: she believes in it, she's convinced that it's part of me. And she would never want to damage part of me because, to her, it would be like hurting all of me; she thinks I'm connected. So I asked her to cut out my tongue.

She was crying in our kitchen. We both cry all the time, it's a habit of ours. We laid down wide blue plastic tarps so the blood wouldn't soak into the concrete floor. I stuck my tongue out and she squeezed it between her thumb

and index finger and pulled lightly; I felt my frenulum stretch, but she couldn't pull hard enough to tear it because the tip was so slippery. Then she pinched the slippery tip between the teeth of the pliers and tightened her grip on the handle. It

hurt. The pliers tasted bitter and metallic and slightly oily. Unlike me, my girlfriend has no childish love of ritual or spurious predilection for ecclesiastical pomp, and her one condition

upon agreeing to cut my tongue out was that we sidestep all decorative symmetry or otherwise unnecessary aesthetic considerations. The job

made her practical and slobbish, like a man. We didn't light scented candles or arrange the silverware in occult geometry or do anything else to suggest

that cutting out my tongue had any meaning. It just

hurt. Light streamed in evenly over the tarps. The enormous white sun shone hot. No one was allowed

out at this time of day; we were safe. She flinched when the blade touched my tongue. Blood began to fill my mouth. I bowed my head

so that it ran into my lap. I didn't want to choke. She sawed.

Tongues are tough, the flesh is rubbery and ungiving. Each stroke
of the knife earned her a few centimeters, until

finally my tongue hung by a thin flap of muscle and she tore it out
by hand. I didn't look at it. I wish I remembered anything

about how it felt, other than the vague sense of overwhelming pain.
I heard a small wet thud as she dropped it onto the tarp. I figured

this was just the kind of thing that brings people closer than ever.
But everyone knows there's a simple paradox whereby any attempt
to bring two things together

pushes them further apart. For example, the closer you get to a
lover, the more you become

aware of how completely incompatible your bodies are, how pro-
liferate the differences in sensitivities and shifts of mood. That's
what closeness comes to be: sharing as little as possible, but sharing
that. And so sometime after I lost my tongue — who knows

how long — I decided that the best way to further degrade our
love was to tell my girlfriend everything, to open

my past to her. I thought that revealing my crimes would drive her
further away. I talked violence; I confessed to a lifetime of malefic
acting out

and deceitful conspiracy. I figured nothing could be worse, more
hurtful and sacrificial, than discovering that the person you love
and feel closest to has been leading a separate life, holding you

at an immeasurable remove, consciously splitting themselves in
two and hiding the other half deep in the half that you thought
you knew. I thought quickly into

my console, and as it transferred my thoughts into my girlfriend's consciousness I thought faster and more associatively, censoring only any self-protective impulse to censorship. In this way, I tried to tell her about the worst things I could remember: robberies, break-ins, beatings,

ritualistic murders, hate crimes, petty lies, arson, rapes, bombings, betrayals, racist diatribes. Stealing her money. Things that did and didn't happen. Things I did and didn't do. Dreams and wishes. The time I played hide and seek

with our two young children, and upon finding them balled-up, clutching their knees and giggling in my bedroom closet, considered slapping them both across the face

for invading my space, for sneaking into daddy's little private room and treating it as if it were just another part of the house and not the only place in the whole world reserved for me alone, a sanctuary too small for me to rest in but nonetheless

symbolic of the continued possibility of a place to rest, someday; but being characteristically unwilling to bear their resentment

I didn't slap either of them, and instead laughed like a delicate old grandmother, almost mutely, because there's something funny, though I can't say what, about small things

trying to appear smaller than they already are in order to go unnoticed by a bigger thing, and I reassured them

that they had found a very clever hiding space this time, and it's lucky I found them because they could have been lost forever, they were hidden so well.

I embellished each of these awful memories. I thought about whatever I hated most in myself and watched my lover's face as the console translated my confessions

directly into her brain. I waited for her wounded reaction, for her console to decode her sad thoughts and send them to me. I wanted proof that I had hurt her. But she didn't think anything

back at me. Her console purred meaninglessly from the back of her head and she only kind of averted her eyes. So I changed course: to be crueler, I thought gentle thoughts. I switched from wallowing in intolerable solipsistic nightmares

to reveling in sweet distant memories and daydreaming about another tender future full of loving kindnesses and warm winter mornings entangled in bed, legs threaded in legs. I figured it would be even worse to follow up my cruel confessions with kind thoughts, because it might interrupt

the righteous pleasure of her anger: my kind thoughts might make her feel guilty for being angry

when I was so clearly trying to bring us closer by confessing, in a true act of love, what I had previously been too afraid or ashamed

to confess. I wanted her guilt to hurt her even more than my cruelty. So I thought nice things, like: I can't live without you. I don't want to live without you. What I love

about your eyes is how they sparkle. (She seems to think about this. I'm getting nervous. I need her to believe me. She's taking so long to reply.) Everybody's eyes sparkle, she said. You can do better than that.